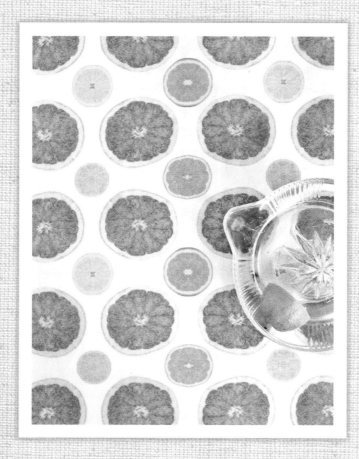

THE Spoonflower HANDBOOK

A DIY GUIDE TO DESIGNING FABRIC, WALLPAPER & GIFT WRAP

STEPHEN FRASER WITH JUDI KETTELER & BECKA RAHN

PHOTOGRAPHY BY JENNY HALLENGREN

STC CRAFT | A MELANIE FALICK BOOK | NEW YORK

CONTENTS

INTRODUCTION

STEPHEN FRASER

By this time, if you are the least bit Internet-savvy and the kind of person interested in crafting and DIY culture, chances are you've heard of Spoonflower. My friend Gart Davis and I started Spoonflower in 2008 with very little money, but an ambitious idea. We wanted to develop the first website to make it possible for people to create and sell their own fabric designs through the Internet.

ABOVE My wife, Kim, and me. We have Kim to thank for inspiring Spoonflower.

Since its modest beginning in a former sock mill in downtown Mebane, North Carolina, Spoonflower has been written about in the *New York Times*, the *Wall Street Journal*, *Better Homes & Gardens*, *Martha Stewart Living*, and *BUST*, as well as in well-known magazines published in Dutch, French, Italian, Spanish, German, and Japanese. The Spoonflower website has been liked and shared, pinned and followed by many thousands of bloggers, Instagrammers, Facebook fans, and Twitterers, and it is safe to say that the once-novel concept of being able to design your own fabric has permanently entered the collective consciousness.

From my standpoint this is enormously satisfying, as you might guess: the stuff of every entrepreneur's dreams. But, like the character in the Talking Heads song who wonders how he managed to land in the middle of the life he is living, I often find myself disoriented in the midst of Spoonflower's success. Is this, in fact, my beautiful website? It seems odd, given my background.

This book is primarily about how to design your own fabric digitally (meaning using a computer), but we also show you how to design for other surfaces, such as wallpaper and gift wrap. Each approach to developing a digital surface design is presented in the context of a handful of projects, which we hope you will want to make and/or use as a jumping-off point for further inspiration. No particular experience is necessary to begin. We've included lessons and projects for novices and experts alike, from the simple (a pillow portrait of your pet) to the complex (an engineered print of a skirt pattern made from one of your own photos). Whether you're a quilter, a crafty parent, a professional artist, or an aspiring fashion designer, there are choices here for you.

We set out to create the most approachable book possible. But I should point out that I'm not a designer. I also can't sew. Neither can my business partner Gart,

ABOVE We showcase Spoonflower designers' work on the tags we include with orders.

with whom I cofounded Spoonflower. In fact, not only were we new to the world of fabric and sewing when we started, neither of us knew a thing about printing or, more broadly, textiles. Asked to play casting director for the ideal founder of Spoonflower, I might have sought out someone dapper, knowledgeable, and engaging: the fashion celebrity and design guru Tim Gunn comes to mind. But, alas, I am no Tim Gunn. People who have observed the state of my desk could reasonably question the wisdom of my involvement in any venture intended to promote a more beautiful or elegant anything. Let's not even bring up my fashion sense. And my partner Gart is, if anything, worse than I am in this respect. So how is it that either of us should have ended up in the business of introducing people to the world of surface design?

Spoonflower was my wife's idea. Unlike me, Kim is an avid sewist (her preferred term) and fabric collector. She's a prolific quilter, enjoys making clothes for our three daughters, and in general displays utter fearlessness when it comes to making almost anything, from soap to homemade Pop-Tarts to hats. Spoonflower came about because, in the fall of 2007, Kim was thinking about making new curtains for our den. One night after work, while I sat on the sofa reading, she described to me her vision for the curtains, which would include fabric with giant

ABOVE Spoonflower is a busy and colorful place! Here are some snapshots of the facility that show our process, from printing to heat-setting to lovingly packaging orders for shipment.

yellow polka dots. The trouble, she explained from somewhere over my shoulder, was that she had not been able to find fabric with yellow polka dots as large as the ones she imagined.

"Wouldn't it be cool," she said, "if there was a place where you could order fabric you designed yourself?" To hear her tell it, I barely looked up from my newspaper. But—and I write this on behalf of husbands everywhere—despite all appearances, I was listening. The wheels were spinning. Partly because of digital technology, we live during a time when the option to customize your own products is, to an astonishing degree, not just common, but expected. Why on earth couldn't a person like Kim design her own fabric?

In January of 2008, not too long after my conversation with Kim about curtains, Gart and I sat down for coffee in Chapel Hill, North Carolina, to talk about the idea of starting a website that would let people create and sell their own fabric. Gart and I had worked together during the initial four years of Lulu.com, the world's first Internet-based self-publishing tool for books, a company founded in 2002. It's where we learned the potential and the pitfalls of self-publishing and print-on-demand. Around the same time, YouTube—which would become the king of all self-publishing sites—was also born.

Although neither of us had much money to invest, we agreed on a course of action that included talking to crafters about the idea and learning more about the technology that would be required to produce print-on-demand fabric. In 2008 there were a few services in the U.S. that offered to print custom fabric for you, but they were, by and large, quite expensive—up to $150 per yard—and none of them had Internet-based business models.

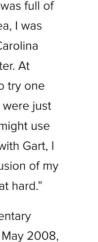

Gart and I were in a great location to learn how to make fabric. As a state whose economy had once relied heavily on textile production, North Carolina was full of textile-related resources. A week after we had coffee to discuss the idea, I was able to go a few miles down the road to Raleigh to visit a lab at North Carolina State University's College of Textiles and see my first digital textile printer. At another institution close by, a not-for-profit called [TC]², I was allowed to try one out. The machinery itself didn't seem complicated. The machines I saw were just big, expensive inkjet printers, larger versions of the sort of device you might use at home to print your photos and documents. In my next conversation with Gart, I effused over a handful of printed fabric samples and relayed the conclusion of my investigations: "We should just buy a printer and try it out. It can't be that hard."

Over the next eight weeks or so, Gart and I hurried to develop a rudimentary version of the service we envisioned. When we launched at the end of May 2008, a special invitation was required to use Spoonflower. Invited visitors could upload a single image, preview it, and add up to three yards of fabric to a shopping cart. Over the summer, working from a waiting list, we approved invitations at a rate of a hundred or so new members per week. In July, our confidence had swelled to such a degree that Gart and I took out a loan to buy our own printer and began to look for a space. In August, we moved into a hot-as-blazes former sock mill, which became our first office. By October, a few months later, we finally allowed the thousands of people on our waiting list to use Spoonflower for the first time. Just a few months later, the *New York Times* ran a piece on Spoonflower on the cover of its Home section titled, "You Design It, They Print It."

The trouble was, we really couldn't print much of anything at that point. The printer on which we had spent our meager savings—along with a second printer we'd

OPPOSITE Spoonflower
community member Andrea
Lauren's constellation
fabric.

purchased just before Christmas—was breaking down. We had more customers and orders every day, but were struggling to print any usable fabric. We knew we had to buy new printers, but because the economy had more or less collapsed at that point, no bank seemed willing to lend us the money. With our printers hobbling along, customers and orders were stacking up and our young startup was struggling to pull together the resources we needed to grow. We got some money from NC IDEA, a local technology grant program. A relative of our ink supplier gave us a personal loan. Kim and I scraped a little more cash out of our home equity.

While things looked pretty grim from a financial standpoint, the Spoonflower community was growing. And our customers, many of whom were following the progress of our little startup soap opera, remained enthusiastic and encouraging. And eventually we did get a loan, we did buy more printers, and we managed to keep the business alive and expanding to meet the demand for custom-printed fabric. Two years after we started, Spoonflower moved from the dusty old mill in Mebane to an office down the road in Durham, where our employees gained the benefit of air conditioning and a break room with a kitchen. Today, our office is a bright and bustling place. We have many printers that run around the clock, churning out fabric and paper designs uploaded to our site from all over the world. Our merry crew has grown to over a hundred. We print wallpaper and gift wrap, as well as fabric, and we have an entire R&D team dedicated to exploring and pushing the limits of the technology so we can extend the power of creative individuals to make beautiful things.

So, what began with an idea for new curtains for our living room has now spun out into yet another, perhaps revolutionary, direction: a book. I am reminded of something someone said to me a couple of months after we launched Spoonflower, when the site still required an invitation to join. The person who said it was Colene McCord, a 70-year-old woman from Knoxville, Tennessee, who was a lifelong friend of my mother. She raised her eyebrows with astonishment when I explained our new business idea. "That's amazing! You know all my life I've wanted to design fabric. Really. When I lie in bed at night and I can't sleep, that's what I do. I design fabric in my mind." Colene is not a designer or an illustrator. She doesn't have skill with a computer. She is a creative person, a person interested in self-expression and beauty and design and pattern. Many, many people share a passion for such expression. It's a thread that runs through many panels of their lives, perhaps showing up as cooking in one person, as gardening in the next. This book is about the joy of making something mingled with the challenge of learning new things. Thanks for picking it up. I can't wait to see what you do with it.

Early on in Spoonflower's history, we developed the idea of holding fabric design contests that anyone could enter. Each week, we would announce a theme, take submissions, and then post all the entries on the same day on our website. Visitors could vote for the designs they liked best. We wanted to make the contest low-key and fun, with a nominal prize of free fabric. We had two goals: first, engage designers by giving them a new challenge each week, and second, showcase designs and photos of printed fabric to inspire new visitors to our site.

At the beginning, the themes of our contests were quite simple—Halloween, Christmas, and so on—but over time they evolved to become more arcane so each contest would be unique. Because we wanted to encourage new work, we also tried to develop themes that would dissuade people from entering designs they'd already created. Surrealist Fruit. Steampunk. Tattoos. Tessellations. Robots. Cocktails. We held a contest for fabric designs created exclusively using crayons, and another for designs featuring fish that used a set palette of colors. We developed a discipline around the weekly contests that included the invention of themes and outreach like a weekly email and Facebook post; an entire section of the site became devoted to administering contests, and we developed code to run it. We've now had hundreds of these contests and have yet to repeat a theme!

A contest devoted to fabric designs was novel, and from the beginning it attracted talented aspiring and experienced designers from all over. Because the voting in Spoonflower contests was open to anyone, it exposed the work of the entrants to lots of new people, some of whom created accounts, "favorited" the designs they liked, left nice comments,

bought yardage in our Marketplace (our onsite shop), or kindly shared the fabrics and artists they discovered through social media. Artists like Deborah van de Leijgraaf (bora), a young mom and former art student from the Netherlands, and Samarra Khaja (sammyk), another young mother and graphic artist who lived in New York, began to acquire fans and followers through the exposure they gained from winning Spoonflower contests. Many people used our contests as a creative challenge, such as Mathew and Matthea den Boer. At the beginning of 2011, this sleepless young couple in Toronto were in the midst of surviving their baby's first year and decided to keep their creative juices alive by entering every Spoonflower contest—one per week—for twelve months. They came in 96th place in the first contest they entered in January. But over the long weeks of winter and spring, the two creatives began to master the art of fabric design. In the first week of August, they won their first contest, which had a coffee theme. They won another before December, when their long year of challenges came to a close.

Eventually, our little community began to attract some big-time attention. Fabric companies much larger than Spoonflower began to follow our contests and to mine the images on our site and on our Facebook and Flickr pages for promising talent. We never saw this as anything but a validation of the idea behind Spoonflower. Unlike a traditional fabric company or retailer we don't have to worry about losing talent because our product, in the end, is not an aesthetic or a set of selected work, but a technology platform that can be used by anyone. We welcome you to try it, too!

CONTEST WINNERS / THEMES

OPPOSITE, TOP TO BOTTOM
LEFT COLUMN
CARYN BENECK (carynikins)
Dim Sum

JODIE PATTERSON (jodielee)
Sewing Celebration

DENIELLE WIEBE (molipop)
African-Inspired

TINA VEY (ottomanbrim)
Horses

CENTER COLUMN
LUCIE DUCLOS (snowflower)
Kuler Spaces

CHAYENNE SAMMONS
(chayenne_sammons)
Aviation

LAURA WRIGHT (laura_the_drawer)
Australian Animals

A. BENEKOS (siya)
Citrus Fruits

RIGHT COLUMN
PATTY RYBOLT (pattyryboltdesigns)
Pies

BRIGITTE JANSEN (mouchette)
Your Town Toile de Jouy

MAAIKE DE VLAS (zandloopster)
Great Barrier Reef

LEAH ROSS (live&cre8)
Floral Coloring Book Wallpaper

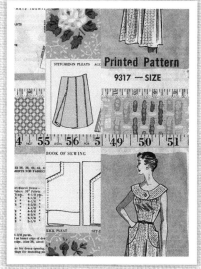

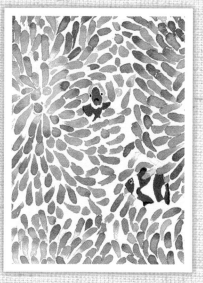

PART 1

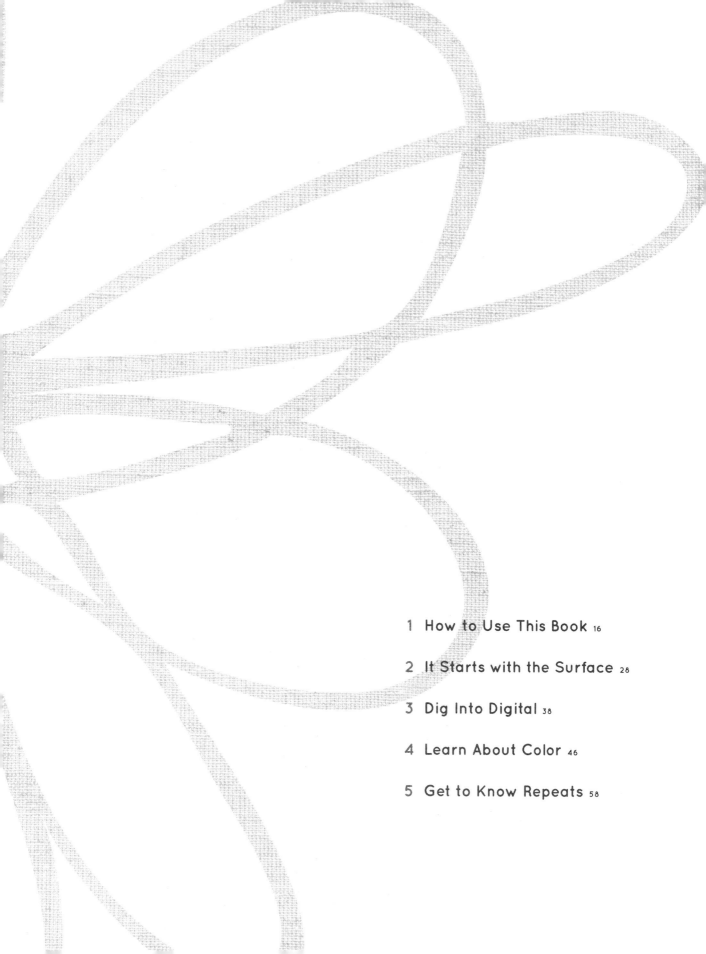

HOW TO USE THIS BOOK
Ready, Set, Get Inspired!

OPPOSITE All you need to get started designing is a computer and an idea.

To decorate the laptop shown here, we printed out a swatch of a sashiko-inspired design by Bonnie Phantasm on peel-and-stick wallpaper. A lot of us at Spoonflower have used the peel-and-stick paper to personalize our laptops, tablets, and phones.

This book assumes that you have used a computer before, that you have some interest in visually representing the world on fabric and paper, and that you like the idea of making things.

We wrote the instructions so that anyone can be successful, including the complete beginner, and we structured the chapters so that skills build upon one another. Of course, if you are already proficient in the ways of design, you can skip around and pull inspiration to do your own thing. Or if you have a specific interest, you can start there and then flip back and forth as necessary to pick up the skills you need. We've included lots of cross-references so you can always find your way. We're very into doing your own thing at Spoonflower. We just want to make sure that we equip you with everything you need to feel empowered as you go.

Spoonflower isn't the only way you can print on demand. There are methods you can try at home, and other services out there as well. Frankly, we're thrilled to see so much interest in surface design, and we always encourage experimentation and innovation. In the end, this book is all about showing you how to make things your own, whether or not you use Spoonflower to generate your materials. To get started, here is an overview of how it all happens.

What is Print-on-Demand?

Having something custom-made for you is not a new idea. But being able to design your own fabric, wallpaper, and gift wrap and have it printed to your specifications *is* a pretty new idea. Spoonflower makes print-on-demand possible by using digital textile printers.

Traditional textile printing has a lot of steps. For each color in a design, an individual silk screen or etching has to be made and mounted on a rolling cylinder, which prints the ink or dye onto the fabric. Fabrics go through a "strike off" process back and forth with the designer, in which small runs are printed to check colors and print quality. Once the designer approves the fabric, custom ink colors are mixed and the factory machines are set up to print thousands of yards from the design. For an individual who only wants to make a few yards of a fabric, the setup time and costs involved in this kind of printing just don't make sense.

Digital textile printers, like we have at Spoonflower, are large-format inkjet printers specially modified to run our fabrics and papers. Unlike conventional textile manufacturing, digital printing requires no setup. There are no screens to make or custom inks to mix. The printer gets the instructions from the computer file you upload to the site and can start printing right away—whether you need a swatch or hundreds of yards (meters) of fabric or paper. This is the essence of print-on-demand: the ability to print exactly what you want, just the way you want it.

How Does Spoonflower Print for Me?

To get custom, one-of-a-kind fabric and papers at Spoonflower.com, we print from your design: that's what this book is all about! In the following chapters, we teach you everything you need to know for all kinds of projects. It doesn't matter if the design is as simple as a little doodle you make on a sticky note and photograph with your phone . . . or as complex as the vector art you will read about in Chapter 10 (page 158)—the basic process is always the same.

Step 1: Create an Account

Creating a Spoonflower account and username allows you to save your designs in your Design Library. And, if you decide to make your designs public, your username is how others will find you. It only takes a minute to set up a Spoonflower account, and it's completely free. Log on at spoonflower.com. Go to "Join" or click on "Log In." If you can't wait to get started, you can even begin the design process without an account if you prefer.

Step 2: Upload Your Design

Once you have your design ready to go, the first step is to upload your artwork to the Spoonflower site using the "Create" link. Uploading involves choosing a file from your computer and clicking the "Upload" button, which you'll see as soon as you click the "Create" link. There are some specifics about how large your file can be and its format, which we outline in the chapters to come.

Step 3: Preview & Choose a Repeat

When the design has finished uploading to your Design Library, you will see a preview of what it looks like when it is repeated, along with a ruler that helps you judge the scale of your pattern (see right). There are several ways you can adjust and customize your design once it is uploaded:

CHOOSE A REPEAT. The design you have uploaded will be tiled—or repeated—to fill the surface. There are five different repeat styles built into our system (we cover them in Chapter 5, beginning on page 58) and you can easily click to switch between them. For example, you can choose to have your image repeat in straight orderly rows (a basic repeat), or you can print a single centered image (a center repeat).

ADJUST THE SIZE. If your image has high enough resolution (page 40), you will be able to click and adjust the size of the repeat tile.

CHANGE COLORS. This tool will help you pick areas of color out of your design and switch them to different colors. Let's say you want blue

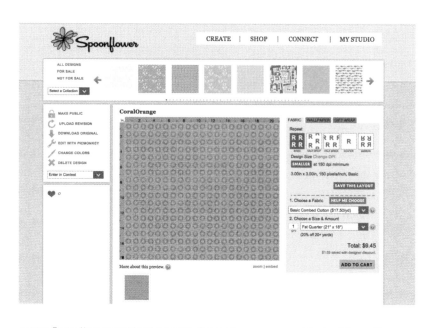

ABOVE Every time you upload a design, it goes to your personal Design Library. From here you can see a preview of how your design will print, make some adjustments, and when ready, place an order.

leaves instead of green leaves in your uploaded design; use the tool to pick the color you want to change and choose a new one with a simple click (see Chapter 4, starting on page 46).

CHANGE PRIVACY. You can toggle between making this design private, so only you can see it (the default), or public, so everyone can join in on the fun. If your skills develop to the point that you'd like to make your designs available for purchase, there is an additional checkbox so you can share a design in the Marketplace (our onsite shop).

MAKE REVISIONS. It's easy to go back and adjust your design later, because it's always saved in your Library.

Step 4: Choose a Surface & an Amount

Each time you order, you can choose to have your design printed on any surface, including more than a dozen fabrics, two types of wallpaper, or two types of gift wrap. Next you choose an amount (swatch, fat quarter, yards, rolls). At this point you will see a preview of what it will look like based on your specifications. Remember that the ruler will show you how your pattern will fill the surface on which you plan to print.

Step 5: Place Your Order

Once you have placed your order, we start printing. Then we cut it, pack it, and ship it directly to you.

How This Book Is Structured

Now that you understand the print-on-demand process, here is how our book will help you turn a spark of inspiration into a package of wonderful fabric or paper waiting at your front door.

PART 1 is all about getting comfortable with digital design. We've organized it into five chapters that are friendly mini-lessons, so that we can walk you through the process step-by-step.

You're reading Chapter 1, **HOW TO USE THIS BOOK**, now, which is about how the print-on-demand process works, the basic equipment you need to get started, and the most important thing you need before you begin—inspiration for your designs.

Chapter 2, **IT STARTS WITH THE SURFACE**, teaches you about the fabrics and other surfaces Spoonflower prints on. We briefly review the different types and sizes, and explain how to start thinking about your surface as a canvas. The surface you print on can influence your design in many ways—an intricate pattern may look great on a smooth surface but not so hot on a textured one, for example—so it's important to think about that as you develop your design.

In Chapter 3, **DIG INTO DIGITAL**, we explore how a design becomes an electronic file. We detail it all from the beginning, step-by-step. It starts with making sure you understand the basics, like pixels and types of digital images. The choices you make about resolution and format (terms defined in the chapter) will change the look and scale of your design.

Chapter 4, **LEARN ABOUT COLOR**, tackles the big, beautiful rainbow of color. The world wouldn't be the same without color, and neither would digital design. But that doesn't mean everything about how color and surface go together is obvious, so we supply you with the information you need. We help you sort through the most common questions and introduce you to a piece of wonderfulness known as the Spoonflower Color Map.

And then you'll be ready for Chapter 5, **GET TO KNOW REPEATS**, where we demystify one of the most fundamental elements of surface design. A repeat is a continuous pattern that fills the surface. We know that repeats intimidate some people, so we start from the beginning and walk you through this concept step-by-step. By the end, you'll be whipping up seamless repeats in your sleep and casually dropping phrases like "half-brick."

PART 2 is when it really gets fun, because we show you how to take what you've learned and apply it to specific projects. With each chapter we introduce more skills and techniques that can be used on their own or mixed and matched. These projects are just a starting point. There are no limits to what you can design and make.

In Chapter 6, **RAID THE JUNK DRAWER: DESIGN WITH FOUND OBJECTS,** we work with collage and odds and ends you might find around the house or in nature. You'll practice using a scanner and creating simple repeats when you make the projects in this section.

In Chapter 7, **THROUGH THE VIEWFINDER: DESIGN WITH PHOTOS,** we show you easy things that you can do with photos using whatever free photo-editing software is already on your computer. But, if you're ready for a bit of adventure, we walk you through some really simple things to try in Adobe Photoshop.

Chapter 8, **FROM PAINT TO PIXELS: DESIGN WITH DRAWINGS, PAINTINGS, AND PRINTS,** shows you some tricks for cleaning up your art after you scan it. This is the point at which you will discover that you don't have to be Michelangelo to work from your original art—even what may begin as a random scribble can be transformed into an interesting design with a few easy-to-use tools.

In Chapter 9, **READ ALL ABOUT IT: DESIGN WITH WORDS, TEXT, AND LAYERS,** we teach you how to manipulate letters, words, and text to create cool projects, and then in Chapter 10, **THE WORLD OF VECTORS: ALL-DIGITAL DESIGNS,** we dive right into design that starts from a blank digital canvas. But by this point, you'll be ready for the challenge. And finally, in Chapter 11, **NO REPEATS NECESSARY: DESIGN CUT AND SEW AND WHOLE CLOTH,** we explore how to design a whole canvas without creating repeats.

Sharing the Love

Spoonflower is a company that lets you design and print your own fabric, wallpaper, and gift wrap. That's what we do. But who we are is a community. That's why we've called upon members of the Spoonflower community to contribute many of the projects and tutorials that appear in this book. From day one, we've wanted to uplift the talent behind Spoonflower—because it is the people who use the site who make it so special. To see more of the work of a designer featured here, go online and search for him or her in our Marketplace, which is our onsite shop. One day we hope to see your designs there as well.

Design Equipment You Need to Get Started

You can spend a lot of money on design equipment and software, but you don't need to do that when you are just getting started. In fact, we thought very carefully and came up with this short list of basics.

+ **COMPUTER** with Internet connection

+ **GRAPHICS SOFTWARE:** This means anything you can use to edit photos or make original digital art. Adobe Photoshop, PicMonkey, Adobe Illustrator, and Gimp are all examples of graphics (or image editing) software. It's really about picking your favorite and what works for you, including the free option that comes standard on your computer. The more expensive software can have lots more options and tools, but the price is higher and you will have a lot to learn. Bottom line: You can make great designs with any graphics program. You can learn and upgrade as you figure out what you need. (See the list of resources on page 206, and also check out Spoonflower. com/design_resources for an even more up-to-date list.)

Each program has a set of tools that help you accomplish tasks such as cropping a photo or resizing an image. Although the symbols and names to denote these tasks can vary slightly from program to program, they all achieve the same result. (Imagine that they all speak the same language but with different accents and dialects.) Once you learn how to recognize each tool, which we teach you how to do in this book, you should be able to sit down with any kind of graphics software and intuitively figure out what to do. If you've never used a graphics program before, check for online tutorials to help you learn the basics. Your local community college may offer classes too.

+ **SCANNER:** This is a device that looks like a flatbed copier but is used to transform what you scan—anything from a document or photo to your child's drawing to a leaf—into a digital file. Technically, this is optional equipment. But scanning is a useful way to transform hand-drawn artwork into digital art. Look for a scanner with a scanning bed size that makes sense for you: a 9 x 12-inch (23 x 30.5 cm) bed is usually large enough, unless you tend to work on larger-format projects, in which case you might want a scanner with an 11 x 17-inch (28 x 43 cm) bed. Look for one designed for scanning photos and text, as there are document scanners that are really only good for print pages. Also, make sure it has options for setting the scan resolution. All-in-one printers also have scanning capabilities, so you can experiment with scanning if you already have this piece of equipment at home or in your workspace.

+ **DIGITAL CAMERA:** This is also optional—but good if you want to work from your own photos. Digital cameras have come so far that there really is no minimum anymore. A smartphone camera provides plenty of pixels, and the quality is really very good.

+ **DIGITAL DRAWING TABLET SUCH AS A WACOM TABLET:** This is a fun tool to add to your repertoire once you get going. A digital drawing tablet allows you to make and edit artwork digitally using a tool similar to writing with pen and paper. There are many styles of tablets; some use a pencil-like stylus to draw directly on the tablet screen, while you can use your fingertip on others.

So What About My iPad?

You can do a lot of the design work on your iPad or other tablet, but you will need a computer when you get to the upload step on the Spoonflower site. Because tablets work on a different kind of file system, there isn't a way to upload a tablet file directly to a web-based interface. That will probably change in the future, but for now you can design away on your tablet and then just transfer your files over to your computer and upload from there. Easy as pie.

Basic Sewing Tools

You don't need everything on this list for every sewing project in this book, but you will need most of them. Have the following on hand when you see "Basic Sewing Tools" in the Materials and Tools list for a project. When required, we add specialty items not on this basic list.

+ Sewing machine
+ Hand-sewing needles
+ Thread
+ Pins
+ Iron and ironing board

+ Scissors (fabric and basic craft)
+ Pinking shears
+ Paper
+ Pencil
+ Ruler and tape measure

Our sewing directions are geared toward DIYers with very basic sewing skills (you've threaded a machine before and understand how to sew lines and curves). If you've never sewn before, but you're a quick study, you might pick up everything you need to know about how to sew from the instructions we give. But to really understand sewing, we recommend consulting a sewing reference book or online site.

Myths and Facts About Using Spoonflower

We've heard some myths about what you need to know to design for fabric and other surfaces digitally. Maybe you've heard them, too. Just in case, let's clear the air.

MYTH: YOU HAVE TO OWN LOTS OF EXPENSIVE EQUIPMENT.

FACT: Chances are you already have what you need to get started. Got a smartphone and a computer? You're set. Add an inexpensive scanner and you have even more options.

MYTH: YOU HAVE TO BE GOOD AT DRAWING.

FACT: Thank goodness this one isn't true. Not all designs begin with sketches. If you're not handy with colored pencils, don't sweat it! Many projects are derived from photographs (like the Infinity Scarf on page 92) or scans (like the First Class Tag on page 72).

MYTH: YOU HAVE TO BE A TECH GEEK.

FACT: Tech geeks are more than welcome. Spoonflower wouldn't be here without them. But you don't have to embrace all things technology to use Spoonflower. And the pieces of technology you do need? We explain how they work step-by-step. With pictures!

MYTH: YOU HAVE TO BE TRAINED IN GRAPHIC DESIGN.

FACT: Nope. Many of our most prolific designers are completely self-taught (meaning they never took a class in school or worked professionally as a graphic designer). At its heart, this book is about teaching. The early chapters introduce tools slowly and logically and explain what you need to know in simple terms.

MYTH: YOU HAVE TO OWN PHOTOSHOP AND ILLUSTRATOR AND BE PROFICIENT IN BOTH.

FACT: For many of the projects, you use can a pencil and paper and your scanner, or simply your camera and free photo-editing software. If you are attempting to use programs like Photoshop and Illustrator for the first time, our instructions explain the specific tools you'll likely need.

MYTH: YOU HAVE TO HAVE LOTS OF TIME ON YOUR HANDS.

FACT: Work (or play) when you have time! Simple designs might only take a matter of minutes to prepare. For example, you could create the design for the Photo Panel Wall Art on page 96 while you brew a cup of tea.

MYTH: YOU HAVE TO BE A COLOR EXPERT.

FACT: Color is really important when designing your surface. So that's why we have an entire chapter about it, and that's why we give you several tools on the site to help you with it. We explain how you can use these tools in Chapter 4 (page 46), and we walk you through the different ways of describing and translating color. But remember that we're all about letting you do your own thing, so you can print in any colors that you want—from your school colors to your daughter's favorite shades of pink and purple. Orange is okay, too!

MYTH: YOU HAVE TO HAVE A BEAUTIFUL AESTHETIC THAT'S MAGAZINE-WORTHY.

FACT: Playful, quirky, vintage, charming, geeky, traditional, funky, futuristic, abstract: All design styles have a home at Spoonflower! What makes our community so strong is that everyone brings a different sense of style with them. Read about our contests on page 12, and you'll see what we mean.

MYTH: YOU HAVE TO MASTERMIND A DESIGN/SEWING/CRAFT BLOG THAT THE WORLD LUSTS OVER.

FACT: We have some fantastic bloggers and makers in the Spoonflower community. If you aspire to that, we are thrilled to be a part of your journey. But everyone's endgame is different, and we are here to empower you on *your* creative path, whatever it may be.

Get Inspired

So, you're excited about the idea of creating your own fabric for a quilt or your own gift wrap for special occasions. All you really need to start is an idea and a willingness to try. We see this in practice every day when people from all over the globe upload amazing designs to Spoonflower. We're constantly inspired just looking at them.

But peering into that beautiful and textured world can also feel intimidating when you're just beginning to understand how to translate your inspirations into a design. Our advice is to start with what you love, discount nothing, and pay attention to everything. Inspiration can truly come from anywhere: the landscape in front of you, a memory, a design aesthetic, a hobby, your kids, traveling, history, your favorite artists, your favorite characters in literature, a classic television show, fashion magazines, nature. It is all there for you, waiting to be transformed into fabric and other surfaces!

If you're not sure how to reflect your personal style or your interests in your designs, turn the page to find out what some of the most prolific members of the Spoonflower community have to say about inspiration. When you see how diverse these folks are—and appreciate how wonderful their designs are, despite being so different—you may begin to hear your own imagination ticking.

LEFT Books are, of course, an endless source of inspiration. You might find ideas in the photos, illustrations, endpapers, typefaces, colors, or text.

SPOONFLOWER DESIGNERS TALK ABOUT INSPIRATION

OPPOSITE, LEFT COLUMN FROM TOP

I am inspired by colors. Light. Different styles. Words. I strive to mimic the atmosphere from whatever inspired me for each design. I was born and raised in Sweden and moved to the United States as an adult. I'm continually inspired by Old Town Stockholm, because it's many hundreds of years old. The buildings have a whimsicality that feels right at home with my sketchy hand-drawn style.

—ANNELIE HERVI (mrshervi)

Movies and television make great inspiration. Using a photo-editing program, I took some iconic scenes from "I Love Lucy" and turned them into simplified images.

—DIANA PIKE (closet_crafter)

This design was inspired by a wall hanging/sconce I saw in an Olive Garden restaurant. There were three terra-cotta pots in a metal wall planter with flowers in it. I sketched out my design on a napkin right there in the restaurant.

—CYNTHIA STRICKLAND (ckstudio80)

I first envision a design on a finished product in a home, and my main inspiration revolves around a narrative. I'm interested in the story that a pattern creates or finishes: Who would use it in their home? Maybe they're well traveled, or maybe they would use it alongside some wonderful vintage finds. The history of a thing, or the thought of its future story, makes it beautiful.

—ANDREA WHALEN (domesticate)

OPPOSITE, CENTER COLUMN FROM TOP

I'm a queer, black, Caribbean woman science-fiction writer. My several communities are both under- and misrepresented in the popular imagination. Part of the joy for me is being able to write us back into history, to imagine our own fantasies and whimsies as an act of intervention. Spoonflower lets me do so visually, in ways that can be both playful and political. I collect historical imagery that speaks to me. I sketch and take photographs. Then I use collage and alteration to remix and re-envision. It's like being a DJ, only with fabric.

—NALO HOPKINSON (nalo_hopkinson)

Currently, there is so much to be inspired by . . . brilliant design, excellent coffee, creative people, unique color palettes, fun DIY projects, stellar mood boards, and living well. Even so, when it's hard to muster a single idea or spark of creativity, I start sketching or doodling on my tablet. This inevitably brings out something interesting that I can build a pattern around. If I am on the go, I jot down notes or a thumbnail sketch to remind me for later.

—HOLLI ZOLLINGER (holli_zollinger)

I am inspired by the perfect days of May and June, painting images of my garden, and the cycle of seasons and color: the blue and purple (crocuses, grape hyacinths, irises, anemones) that come after the Toronto snow, followed by white and yellow (daffodils, tulips) and by pink (peonies, poppies, sweet peas), then white. Finally, I'm inspired by my mother, who has always brought color to my life.

—VIVIAN DUCAS (cest_la_viv)

My goal is to tell a story by manipulating traditional patterns and injecting them with characters inspired by books, dreams, nature, and, well, life.

—CATE ANEVSKI (cateanevski)

OPPOSITE, RIGHT COLUMN FROM TOP

This is my ode to the breathtakingly beautiful handmade tradition of Mexican Otomi embroidery. So much time and care is taken when creating all of the needlework flora and fauna details. I wanted to not only honor it with my design, but offer up a printed version that would not be wince-inducing to cut up and sew into something, because embroidered Otomi designs are too wonderful to do that to!

—SAMARRA KHAJA (sammyk)

Traveling to colorful countries all over the world is a great starting point for inspiration. But even cultures that I haven't seen with my own eyes can be inspiring. I love doing research because it feels a little bit like going on a trip. In some of my designs this inspiration is very evident; in others it's less so, but it's always there even if just in the choice of colors.

—INE BEERTEN (zesti)

This design was inspired by the camping trips I used to take with my family as a little girl. I loved those getaways. We set up our tents on large green fields of grass and listened to music next to the campfire. Sometimes a guitar, sometimes a little boom box playing electronic '80s tunes. I always imagined wild animals in the trees behind our tents. I travel a lot nowadays and visit new places and experience new cultures—these trips are an inspiration I translate into my illustrations and design work—but it all started out with those family camping trips.

—MAIKE BOOT (littlesmilemakers)

My love for texture and appreciation of all things knit by hand (despite my inability to knit much of anything at all), inspired this fun pattern that features simple lines and a limited color palette.

—SAMANTHA COTTERILL (mummysam)

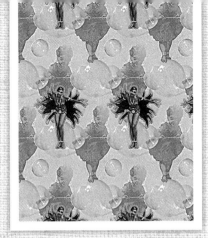

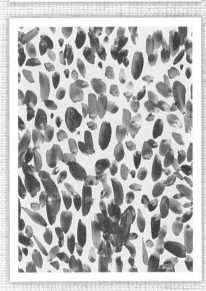

IT STARTS WITH THE SURFACE

OPPOSITE The same pattern can look very different based on the surface it is printed on. The floral design featured on different fabrics here was designed by Jiah Harrison of Australia.

Spoonflower originally printed on only one surface: literally, one kind of fabric, quilting-weight cotton. Now we print on a wide range of fabrics in varying widths, weights, and textures. Want eco-friendly canvas for cushions? Check. How about stretchy knit for yoga wear? Got you covered. And of course, we still offer versatile quilting-weight cotton as well as several organic fabrics. We also offer gift wrap in two different finishes and two kinds of wallpaper, water-activated and peel-and-stick.

The skills you need to create your digital design don't change based on the surface, but a good understanding of the characteristics of the different surfaces will help you to choose the best one to achieve the results you are seeking.

Basic Combed Cotton

Heavy Cotton Twill

Cotton Silk

Cotton Poplin

org. cotton Knit

organic cotton Sateen

Silk

Spoonflower

swatches
WWW.SPOONFLOWER.COM

DESIGN YOUR OWN | FABRIC
WALLPAPER
GIFT WRAP

TEXTURE

Texture refers to how a surface looks and feels. It also helps determine how a design will look when it is printed. For example, if you are printing a photograph on fabric and you want it to print very crisply and clearly, you might choose a basic quilting-weight cotton. If you'd like a hazier look, you might go with heavy cotton twill or canvas. In the photos at right you can see one child's portrait printed on a variety of fabrics. One look isn't necessarily better than the other—it's just important that you understand how texture will influence your result so you can choose according to your goals. To familiarize yourself with the different textures of the fabrics and papers we offer, you may want to get one of our swatch books (page 33).

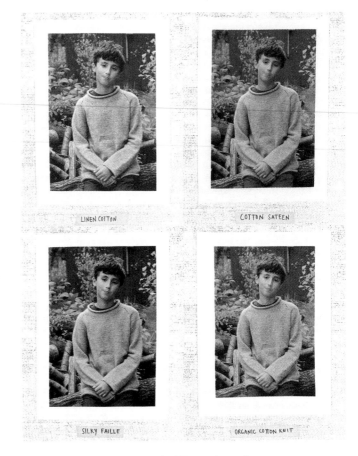

LINEN COTTON

COTTON SATEEN

SILKY FAILLE

ORGANIC COTTON KNIT

ABOVE The same image will look different depending on the texture of the fabric it is printed on.

DRAPE & STRUCTURE

Some kinds of fabric are very soft and flowing, and some have more body or structure, which helps them hold a shape or keep a fold. We chose silk crepe de chine to give the Infinity Scarf on page 92 a soft, flowing drape. Conversely, for the Citrus Dish Towels on page 108, we chose the stronger, stiffer linen-cotton canvas. See page 34 to learn more about choosing a fabric that is appropriate for the use you've got in mind.

RIGHT & WRONG SIDES

For all of the Spoonflower surfaces, the right side is the printed side. The wrong side is the unprinted side of the fabric or gift wrap and the adhesive side of the wallpaper. Although you can't change what the wrong side looks like—varying shades of white depending on the surface—you should be aware of this characteristic. For example, when you're sewing, the wrong side of the fabric could be visible in some projects, so plan accordingly.

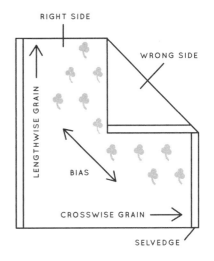

FIGURE 1 Here's an overview of basic fabric terminology. We print your designs along the crosswise grain.

WIDTH

Spoonflower's fabrics and surfaces have a printable area that ranges from 24 to 58 inches (61 to 147 cm) wide; test swatches and fat quarters are smaller.

The width of the surface is important to consider when you're developing a project; for example, we wanted our Doppelganger Dog Pillow on page 105 to be a fun, cuddly, economical project that we could print on a fat quarter of linen-cotton canvas that is 27 x 18 inches (68.6 x 46 cm). If that's your goal for this cut-and-sew project too, then your dog design can't be larger than the dimensions of the fat quarter. Of course, it's fine if you want your pooch to be bigger than our Ruby, but then you will have to print on a full yard (.9 m) of fabric instead of a fat quarter. Knowing the width of your surface helps you scale your design correctly from the beginning.

SELVEDGE

The selvedges are the finished edges that run the length of the fabric yardage; we can't print on them, so we don't include them in the "printable area" we list for our fabrics. If you're just starting to learn about fabric, these finished edges help you quickly identify the direction of the grain (see Figure 1), a quality that's important when you design a print and also when you sew.

GRAIN

Grain refers to the direction of the fibers in the fabric or paper. For fabric, the lengthwise grain runs the length of the fabric and is parallel to the selvedge. The crosswise grain runs perpendicular to the selvedge. Spoonflower's fabrics and papers are all printed aligned with the crosswise grain. This means that the repeat of your design will be printed from one selvedge to the other (see Figure 2). But you can also decide to rotate the design 90° before you upload it so it runs along the lengthwise grain (see Figure 3). It's a design choice at heart and is totally up to you.

However, the direction that your design prints can affect your project, especially if your design has a specific orientation (a "directional" print). This is particularly important if you're making clothing because the pattern pieces for a garment are usually laid out along the lengthwise grain, the most stable direction. Compare Figures 2 and 3 to see how directional prints look when placed differently along the fabric's grain.

BIAS

Fabric also has a bias grain, which runs diagonally. When you cut woven fabric on the bias, it has more stretch and drape than fabric you cut with the straight grain. That's why garments cut on the bias are so wonderful: they drape very nicely and tend to hug your curves. If you are designing fabric for a project you want to cut on the bias, you will definitely need to think about how your design will work when it's cut diagonally.

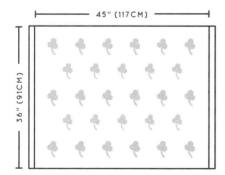

FIGURE 2 This directional pattern is printed along the crosswise grain.

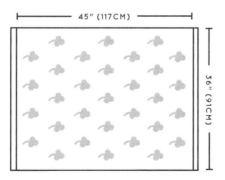

FIGURE 3 This is the same pattern used in Figure 2, but printed along the lengthwise grain.

How Are Fabrics and Papers Sold at Spoonflower?

You can buy a . . .

SWATCH BOOK

This book contains a small square (approximately 4 x 4 inches [10 x 10 cm]) of each of our fabrics plus wallpaper and gift wrap samples. Check it out in the photograph on page 29.

FABRIC SWATCH

A swatch is 8 inches (20 cm) square. It's always a good idea to order a swatch of fabric before you purchase several yards (meters) to make sure your design prints the way you envisioned and that the fabric itself has the qualities you want. Swatches are great for projects, too. What can you do with a square that small? You'd be amazed—see "A Square Isn't Just a Square" on page 37!

FAT QUARTER OF FABRIC

A fat quarter is half of the width and half of the length of a yard (36 inches [91 cm]) of fabric. Our fat quarters will vary slightly in size based on the width of the fabric. For example, for a yard of fabric that is 44 inches wide x 36 inches long (110 x 91 cm) wide, a fat quarter is 22 x 18 inches (56 x 46 cm).

YARD OF FABRIC

A yard is 36 inches (91 cm) in length. The widths vary from 42 to 58 inches (107 to 147 cm), depending on the fabric. Spoonflower will sell you as many whole yards as you want, but the only fractional yards we sell are swatches and fat quarters (Figure 4). If you need 2½ yards (2.3 m) for a project, you need to round up and buy 3 yards (2.7 m). Or, you might study the cutting layout to see if 2 yards (2 m), plus 2 fat quarters, will work. (And although we've provided metric conversions throughout this book for our international friends, note that we only sell our surfaces in U.S. customary units, meaning inches and yards.)

OTHER SURFACES

Here is how we sell our paper products (Figure 5).

+ For wallpaper, Spoonflower sells swatches (24 x 12 inches [61 cm x 30.5 cm]) and standard rolls (24 x 144 inches [61 cm by 366 cm]). Wallpaper is also sold in custom-length rolls.

+ For gift wrap, rolls are 26 x 72 inches (66 x 183 cm).

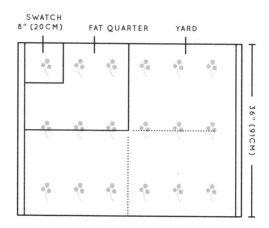

FIGURE 4 Spoonflower's fabrics are sold in three different ways.

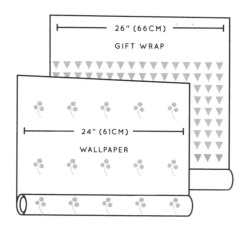

FIGURE 5 Our papers are available by the roll (wallpaper and gift wrap) or swatch (wallpaper).

OPPOSITE We printed a few yards of Andrea Lauren's constellation fabric to use as a cloth for an outdoor table. We just cut it to fit the table without even hemming. We chose Spoonflower's Eco Canvas because it is heavy-duty and wipes clean easily. Making a tablecloth like this is an easy way to introduce a theme at any party, indoor or out.

IT STARTS WITH THE SURFACE

WHAT ARE YOU GOING TO MAKE WITH THAT?

Think of choosing a surface as putting together a puzzle: First you have to consider how your design will look (remember, a design will look different on a textured surface versus a smooth one, for example), and then you have to think about whether the surface will work for the project you want to make (a canvas bag will have more structure than a poplin one, so if it's structure you want, choose canvas).

We asked Emma Jeffery, one of the Spoonflower community's most prolific sewers and crafters, to leverage her experience using Spoonflower's myriad surfaces and share her best tips for choosing the right one for a project. While specific surfaces may come and go as we revise our inventory, we will always have some available in the categories shown below and Emma's suggestions will still apply.

QUILTING-WEIGHT FABRICS

(such as basic cotton and Kona®)

WHAT YOU'LL LOVE ABOUT THESE FABRICS: They're soft, durable, and breathable, and nearly any design looks good printed on them.

WHAT YOU CAN DO WITH THESE FABRICS: Make almost anything! The possibilities for these versatile fabrics are almost limitless, including:

+ Quilts and appliqué

+ Children's clothing

+ Casual shirts and dresses that don't require stretch

+ Home accents

+ Purses, pouches, and bags

+ Toys

WOVEN CLOTHING-TYPE FABRICS

(including poplin or sateen)

WHAT YOU'LL LOVE ABOUT THESE FABRICS: They are easy to work with and machine-wash well. Their textures vary from slightly thicker and coarse (twill and poplin) to more luxe and shiny (sateen).

WHAT YOU CAN DO WITH THESE FABRICS:

+ Make fitted or tailored clothing from sateen and poplin. They are also good choices for decorating or apparel projects that need more structure.

+ Stitch a great blouse or dress from sateen.

LIGHTWEIGHT FABRICS

(like satin or faille)

WHAT YOU'LL LOVE ABOUT THESE FABRICS: They drape beautifully and are delicate to the touch, but are also fairly durable and easy to sew. If you're using them to make clothing, you might want to consider lining the garment.

WHAT YOU CAN DO WITH THESE FABRICS:

+ Make scarves, skirts, blouses, dresses, lingerie, and pajamas, since these fabrics are on the sheer side.

+ Try them for home decorating, soft furnishings, or quilts—they can bring a unique look and feel to these accessories.

HEAVYWEIGHT FABRICS

(such as linen-cotton canvas or eco-canvas)

WHAT YOU'LL LOVE ABOUT THESE FABRICS: They are durable, hard-wearing fabrics that resist creases and wrinkles and wash well—and they only improve as they are used and washed repeatedly.

WHAT YOU CAN DO WITH THESE FABRICS:

+ Sew them into table linens such as tea towels and tablecloths, because they are super-absorbent.

+ Redecorate your home. Because they have a heavier weight and provide more structure, they are well suited for upholstery projects and cushions.

+ Make heavyweight apparel such as coats and jackets; they're also good choices for more structured bags and totes.

KNIT FABRICS

(including jersey, interlock, and performance knits)

WHAT YOU'LL LOVE ABOUT THESE FABRICS: They stretch! This makes them great for clothing because you don't have to worry so much about the accuracy of the fit of your finished item; also, knits don't fray (which means you don't have to finish seams). A couple of tips to keep in mind: for synthetic knits, iron on a low heat setting; check your sewing machine's manual for suggestions about simple adjustments to the settings for sewing with knits.

WHAT YOU CAN DO WITH THESE FABRICS:

+ Make garments that need stretch, such as tees, dresses, shirts, blouses, athletic wear, undies, and baby clothes.

+ Try them for blankets, soft toys, and beanie hats, too.

WATER-ACTIVATED & PEEL-AND-STICK WALLPAPER

WHAT YOU'LL LOVE ABOUT THESE SURFACES: They are easy to mount and totally removable.

WHAT YOU CAN DO WITH THESE SURFACES:

+ Create custom wall treatments.

+ Change the look of a room, piece of furniture, or object without having to commit to a more permanent solution.

+ Cut to size or shape with scissors, a craft knife, or a die-cutting machine.

GIFT WRAP

WHAT YOU'LL LOVE ABOUT THIS SURFACE: It opens up a million possibilities for paper crafting. It's thick, high-quality paper, which can be used for all kinds of creative purposes, without the worry that it will easily rip or tear.

WHAT YOU CAN DO WITH THIS SURFACE:

+ Wrap gifts (obviously)!

+ Make gift bags or cover books.

+ Use for decoupage projects.

+ Fold for origami.

+ Use in scrapbooking and collage.

To Prewash or Not?

There are a lot of opinions about whether or not to prewash fabric before you sew something. Our suggestion—if you plan to wash after you sew, you should wash before you sew. Almost every fabric will shrink to some degree when it's laundered, and prewashing the fabric allows you to plan accordingly.

Washing also affects the fabric's hand, or feel, because it removes any starch or sizing leftover from the manufacturing process. If the hand is important to the success of your project, consider ordering swatches and laundering them so you can judge any change for yourself and proceed accordingly.

On a practical note, we recommend that you use phosphate-free detergents to wash your fabrics.

A SQUARE ISN'T JUST A SQUARE

A question we often get asked is: "What can I do with a swatch?" A swatch is a great way to test out your design and especially your colors. But that's not all a swatch is good for! Here are some ideas from Diane Gilleland on how you can create with your fabric and paper swatches. Diane is one of our favorite guest bloggers at Spoonflower and one of the craftiest people we know.

FABRIC SWATCHES
8 x 8 inches (20 x 20 cm)

+ Cut an 8-inch (20 cm) circle and run a gathering stitch all the way around. Pull that stitch to make a little bag. Stuff it firmly, tie off the thread, and add a big button to cover the opening. Now you have a pincushion!

+ One swatch makes four coasters or one mouse pad—glue the fabric to the cork with Mod Podge or spray adhesive. If the fabric is a light color, you may want to apply some gesso to the cork before adding the fabric to avoid show-through (that's what we did for the mouse pad at left).

+ A "mug rug" is a large coaster that holds your coffee cup and a cookie. And a fabric swatch is the perfect size for a mug rug: just add some batting and backing fabric.

+ Iron some fusible web to the back of a swatch and then cut out appliqués. Fuse and stitch the appliqués to bags, napkins, bibs, tea towels, etc.

+ Cut a swatch into several strips, sew them end to end, hem the raw edges, and you have a pretty hatband. Stitch them onto some cotton belting and add some D-rings for a sweet belt.

+ You can make six to eight covered buttons from a fabric swatch, depending on the size of the buttons. For the buttons in the photo at left we used a fabric design made up of a grid of patterns; the end result was a varied but cohesive set of buttons.

+ Use a swatch to make a cool pocket on a bag, skirt, or top.

+ Small canvases become instant wall art with a covering of fabric. That is what we did with the repeat patterns on page 59.

WALLPAPER SWATCHES
24 x 12 inches (61 x 30.5 cm)

+ A single wallpaper swatch can cover up to eight double switch plates or twelve single ones. We used the same pattern for our buttons and our switch plates.

+ Cover a standard composition book with water-activated wallpaper by simply moistening the wallpaper and sticking it to the cover (as we did for the black-and-white notebook at left). You'll have enough left over to cover a mini notebook, too. If the paper you are applying is a light color, you may want to apply some gesso to the notebook first to avoid show-through.

+ Make a simple bookmark by cutting a 2 x 6-inch (5 x 15 cm) strip of wallpaper and machine-sewing around all four sides with a decorative stitch. One swatch makes up to twenty-four bookmarks, so you can give lots away as gifts!

+ Fold wallpaper or gift wrap to make pretty envelopes in any size you like. Do an online search for envelope templates. We created two different envelope styles, as you can see in the photo at left.

+ Wrap a strip of wallpaper around a pillar candle or a glass votive holder for a decorative touch.

+ Glue wallpaper to some heavy chipboard. Cut along the design lines, punch a hole, and add some ribbon. Now you have some fancy gift tags or tree ornaments.

OPPOSITE Clockwise from top left: Envelope patterns by Leanne Hatch, button and switchplate patterns by Eleanor Ramsay, mousepad pattern by Isabelle Kunz, notebook pattern by Andrea Lauren.

3

DIG INTO DIGITAL

OPPOSITE We made
this cotton sateen pillow
following the Portrait
Pillow instructions on page
101. Instead of printing a
family photo, we printed
a pixellated version of the
hyacinth photo on page 97.

Some people feel intimidated when they hear the term "digital design." We admit—it sounds kind of fancy and technical. But we're here to break it down for you so that you understand how accessible it is to anyone with a computer. Put simply, digital design is the process you use to transfer an idea from your head to a computer screen and how you then manipulate it to make it look the way you want.

Your design may start on paper, from a photograph, or from a graphics program. No matter how it arrives on the screen in front of you, you have the power to transform it in a multitude of ways. In this chapter, we focus on the basic concepts that will help you as you get started. In the chapters that follow we explore the many techniques you can use to manipulate the design.

A Basic Digital Vocabulary

Here are some important definitions for terms we use throughout the book. To get started, we keep these definitions pretty simple. At the end of most of the entries is a cross reference to another page where you can get more in-depth information when you're ready.

PIXELS

Pixels are tiny bits of information that make up digital image files. Think of pixels as Legos or puzzle pieces—a collection of many units that work together to make a bigger design. On a computer monitor, they generally look like little squares but are often referred to as dots, too. (Read more about them on page 41, because they're really important!)

RESOLUTION

Resolution is the number of pixels or dots displayed per inch. It is often labeled ppi (pixels per inch) or dpi (dots per inch). We use dpi when we reference the printing process, which is customary. When you look at an image on a computer screen or as it is printed on a piece of paper or fabric, the pixels are represented by dots of light or ink. The more pixels you have in a digital image, the more versatility you have when changing its size or printing it (see the Pixel Equation on page 42 for more detail).

FILE

A computer file is a collection of data. While "file" is often used to describe a text file, an image is stored in a file, too.

There are different file types (such as .jpg or .tif) because there are different ways to organize that information so the computer can store and understand it. (Learn more about file types on page 45.)

CANVAS

In the digital sense, we use the term "canvas" to describe the new file that we create to start a design in a graphics program. A canvas is defined in terms of pixels, so you create a new file that is x number of pixels tall by y number of pixels wide.

RESIZE

Resizing a design involves changing its dimensions; in the book, we use this term when we are making an image smaller. By contrast, we use the term "scaling" to describe making an image larger, although you may see these terms used interchangeably elsewhere. We resize images in the projects in Chapter 7.

SCALE

Scaling is a technique used to make a design larger without compromising its quality; it involves some easy math that is based on the Pixel Equation (page 42). We scale images in the projects in Chapter 6.

SCAN

Scanning is the method used to convert a hand-drawn image or other object to a digital format using a tool called a scanner.

RASTER IMAGE

Raster images are made up of pixels arranged in a grid or pattern. When you look at a raster image up close, you will see each individual pixel. A digital photograph is a familiar example of a raster image.

VECTOR IMAGE

Instead of a grid of pixels, vector images are based on lines, curves, and other geometric shapes created from mathematical formulas in a computer program. (Read more about vector images, and the difference between vector and raster images, on page 44.)

All About Pixels

Digital images on your computer or your camera are essentially big collections of those little dots of data, pixels. Although your eye views it as a whole, a digital image is actually made up of hundreds, thousands, millions of dots even, depending on how big the image is. The more dots per inch, the sharper the image.

When you scan a piece of artwork, create a raster image (page 44) in a graphics program, or take a photograph with a digital camera, you are creating a file with an exact number of pixels. An 8-megapixel iPhone camera creates a file with 8,000,000 pixels every time you click the button. When you make a new file in a graphics program, you can choose the number of pixels wide and the number of pixels tall you want that file to be.

PIXELS AND PRINTING

When you look at pixels on your computer or tablet screen, you see little dots of colored light. Your printer translates pixels into dots of ink, just as our big printers do at Spoonflower. The number of pixels in your image can have a big influence on the printed result, both in terms of quality and size.

If you don't know it already, it's easy to find out the number of pixels in your image, because you can open it in a graphics program and use the Image Size or Resize tool to see its size; you can also look at the information about the file in the Finder (Mac) or Explorer (Windows).

For many smooth printing surfaces such as photographic paper, 300 dpi (dots per inch) is the desired resolution. But Spoonflower uses a default resolution of just 150 dpi because our textured surfaces take less ink; this means your file sizes can be smaller and your design will upload faster, too.

150 DPI

For the projects in this book, we always start with 150 dpi as the resolution, because that is the resolution for Spoonflower's printers. Although we explain how you can manipulate the resolution for different effects on page 43, 150 dpi is aways our baseline.

The Pixel Equation

To figure how best to achieve a desired result, often you will need to complete the Pixel Equation. There are three variables in this equation: number of pixels in the image, resolution (ppi or dpi), and size in inches of the image. As long as you know two of them, you can figure out the third, using one of the three versions of the equation below:

VERSION 1: Pixels ÷ resolution (ppi or dpi) = size in inches

VERSION 2: Size in inches x resolution (ppi or dpi) = pixels

VERSION 3: Pixels ÷ size in inches = resolution (ppi or dpi)

Let's use a scenario to explore the relationship between pixels, image size, and resolution that is so important when you print: Let's say you have a photo of a tape measure that is 900 pixels wide and you would like to print one large image of it at 36 inches, to fill a yard of fabric. To determine if you have enough pixels to print it clearly at that size we use the Pixel Equation (see left).

Since we know the number of pixels in the image and the resolution needed, let's do the math using version 1 of the equation (Figure 1):

900 PIXELS ÷ 150 DPI = 6 INCHES

But 6 inches is not what you had in mind. Don't despair; here's how the formula can help you. Since you need your design to be larger, you need to start with more pixels. This is the key to working with pixels—you must think before you scan, snap, or create, because you can't manufacture more pixels. It would be great if you could simply enlarge your 900-pixel image and have it print clearly at the size you want . . . but you can't, even though it may appear otherwise.

If you play around with your photo-editing program, you may come across a little box where you can type in any number of pixels you want to seemingly make an image bigger. But it's really an illusion, because to do so, the editing program pulls all of your original pixels apart and then tries to fill in the gaps between them by guessing what color should go where. That's why your image could end up looking blurry or jagged, the quality described as "pixelated." So while it is easy to delete pixels to make an image smaller, you can't reliably create pixels to make an image larger if pristine clarity is what you're seeking.

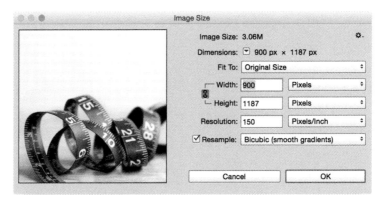

FIGURE 1 The tape measure photo is 900 pixels wide. Remember the pixel equation shows us that 900 pixels at 150 dpi will give us an image that is 6 inches (15 cm) wide.

All that said, let's use version 2 of the Pixel Equation to determine how many pixels the tape measure image needs to be printed at 36 inches, which is your goal.

36 INCHES X 150 DPI = 5400 PIXELS

So to get the result you want for this giant tape measure design, you would need to start with an image that is 5400 pixels wide. There are lots of ways to make an image suitable for printing when you know what size you need. You can start by creating a new file exactly to your specifications— by designing it with software, taking a photo at a high-quality setting, creating original artwork, or cropping and resizing a larger image—and you will learn all of those techniques step-by-step as you work through the projects in the coming chapters.

As you read through the book, you will see that we use one of the variations of the Pixel Equation in almost every project. Sometimes it makes sense to approach a design through intuition and trial-and-error, but sometimes you need to have a little more control. Understanding the Pixel Equation lets you make intentional artistic choices to help you create the design you really want.

Playing with Pixels

You can make an aesthetic choice to create a pixelated look, as we show below and on the pillow on page 39. We manipulated our image by reducing the number of pixels but leaving the image size the same (18 inches [46 cm]). The original photo (Figure 2) was first resized from 150 ppi to 2 ppi, which made the pixels appear as large squares (Figure 3). We then rescaled it once more back to 150 ppi so that it would print at 18 inches. Learn about resizing on page 90.

FIGURE 2 The original hyacinth photo is 2700 pixels x 2700 pixels. If we print it at 150 pixels per inch, it will be 18 inches (46 cm) square.

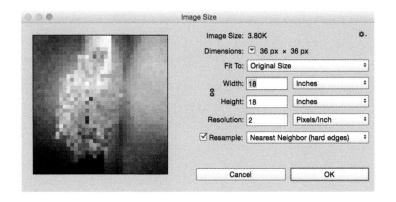

FIGURE 3 When we reset the resolution to 2 pixels per inch, we create a pixellated effect because each pixel appears as a large square.

Raster Images vs Vector Images

Raster and vector images are both considered digital images, but vector images are not based on pixels. Vector images are based on points, lines, curves, and polygons defined by the graphics program and described as mathematical formulas. When you are ready to print a vector-based image, you choose the size you want to print, and the program (such as Adobe Illustrator) translates the vectors, lines, and shapes into a collection of pixels that the printer can understand. Unlike raster images, vector images are scalable up and down to almost any size without affecting how they look, because you only create the pixels when you need to use them, so to speak.

Many designers work with both kinds of images, depending on what they are trying to accomplish. Neither is better than the other: They are just used differently to accomplish different looks and effects.

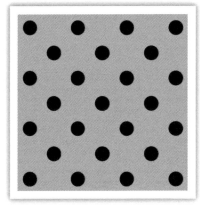

Though both of these designs feature polka dots, they were created in very different ways. Emily Sanford's Polkadots in Water (far left) is a raster image: the original artwork was done in watercolor and scanned. By contrast, Andrea Whalen's Polkas in Sheer Stockings (near left) is a vector image, created entirely on the computer in a graphics program.

ABOUT RASTER IMAGES

+ Photographs or scans are raster images.

+ Raster images allow much more fine detail. Because you can set every pixel to a different color, you have a lot more control over shading, texture, and depth. You can reproduce effects like watercolor painting or shiny chrome through manipulation of the colors, pixel by pixel.

+ Adobe Photoshop, PicMonkey, and Gimp all work primarily with raster images.

ABOUT VECTOR IMAGES

+ Vector images are best for producing precise shapes and smooth lines and curves. Geometric patterns are easy to do with vector-based images.

+ Vector images deal with color much more simply than raster images. Each line or shape can be filled with a color or gradient and it is easy to change colors. However, it is much more difficult to create effects like shadows or organic textures.

+ Business logos are often created using vector graphics so they can be scaled to any size without losing quality.

+ Adobe Illustrator and Inkscape work primarily with vector images.

Graphic File Types

The last topic in our digital overview involves file type, which describes the way that the computer organizes and saves the millions of pixels it has to keep track of in a digital file. Each graphics program uses different file types, and each works a little differently.

When you are working on a new design in a graphics program, you will be prompted to choose a file type when you save it. You will have many options, depending on the program, and you can save versions of your design in a variety of file formats. Spoonflower is set up to accept several different kinds (described below), but we recommend uploading your designs as a .jpg or a .png file.

Some programs, like Photoshop and Illustrator, also have their own file formats that are designed to preserve all of your working layers, history, and color palettes. These .psd or .ai files are not directly uploadable to Spoonflower because they contain too much extra information for the printers; however, they are a great way to save your design as you are editing and working on it. Once you have the design finished, you can save it or export it as a .jpg file (or any of the others listed below) and upload to Spoonflower.

Here is an overview of some of the file types we accept:

+ .jpg or .jpeg is probably the most universal file type. It is a standard format for images and graphics. Most cameras and scanners are set up to create .jpg files by default.

+ .png is also a common file type that is capable of preserving sharpness and fidelity; it can be better for line art designs.

+ .tif or .tiff is also a standard format for images and graphics. File sizes tend to be larger than other formats due to less compression of data.

+ .gif files are often used for web design, as they can support transparency and animation, but they can be desirable for computer-generated images with a limited color palette.

LEARN ABOUT COLOR

At Spoonflower, we get a lot of questions. But the most common one is this: "How do I get the colors I see on my monitor to match the colors on my printed fabric or paper?" A color should just be a color, right? Well, the answer isn't quite so simple.

On a screen, color is made from light. But when you print it out using ink or dye, the color is made from pigments. The color of the fabric or paper—and even the color of the light in the room—can influence what the color looks like to the eye.

Every device—a monitor, printer, scanner, camera, and even a .jpg file itself—has a set of colors that it can work with, called the color gamut. It's like a crayon box. Your monitor might have the 64-color box; your printer might have the 24-color box. Each time you ask it to show a color, it pulls out a crayon from its box.

Of course, computers don't name colors "Cornflower Blue" or "Yellow Orange" like crayon manufacturers. Instead, they label them with numbers. There are different ways to number or describe colors; these are called color modes, and you might recognize some of the abbreviations, like **RGB**, **CMYK**, **LAB**, or **HSB**.

Color Modes

Each of the color modes uses its own system or language to describe a color. For example, **RGB** gives values for the amount of red, green, and blue light that make up a color. **CMYK** refers to the percentage of cyan, magenta, yellow, and key (black) used to build a color. **HSB** refers to hue, saturation, and brightness. **LAB** defines a color by the lightness (the "L" stands for light) and its position on an A and B axis of red-green and blue-yellow (that's the "A" and "B").

Whenever you are working in a program that lets you pick colors (such as Adobe Photoshop, Microsoft Word, or one of the free design programs available), you'll be presented with a palette (a panel of functions) with color options. For example, you can look at the Color Picker tool in Photoshop (see Figure 1) and see how it displays each of the different color modes.

Color Profiles

The color gamut from your device (the "crayon box" of colors you have available) and the color mode (the way of describing those colors) create what is called a color space for that particular piece of equipment. Since your monitor and the Spoonflower printer don't have the same color space, they need to have a way to communicate with one other. So, there is a translator (a set of rules) between the two called a color profile. It works something like this: "If I ask for Cornflower Blue and the printer doesn't have that color in the box, then use Sky Blue instead." Color profiles also take into account the ways of producing colors you have (i.e., pigments or dyes), and the kind of paper or fabric you are printing on.

There are lots of ways to write these rules for translating colors between devices. Manufacturers of digital cameras and photo printers build in color profiles that emphasize contrast (the difference between dark and light) and saturation (the intensity) of your colors overall, because that is very visually appealing (in other words, it makes your photos look better). Spoonflower uses a set of rules based on relative rendering, which changes as little as possible about your file, adjusting only the colors in your gamut that aren't available in Spoonflower's printers and leaving the rest of the colors as they are. This ensures that photographs and surface designs print as accurately as possible each time you order, and that colors will stay consistent when printing on the same fabric. All of these adjustments happen automatically when you upload your file; you don't need to do anything.

FIGURE 1 This pretty light blue-green can be described in each color mode: RGB (R138 G199 B198) or its "shorthand" hexadecimal code #8ac7c6; LAB (75 -30 -9); and so on.

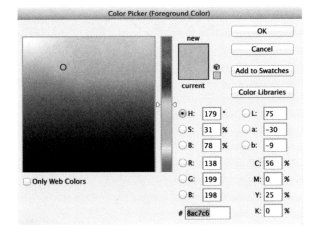

Matching Colors

We haven't forgotten about the original question, "How do I get the colors I see on my monitor to match the colors on my printed fabric or paper?" Here are two solutions.

You can calibrate your monitor to show specific colors as accurately as possible. Using a tool called a colorimeter and some special software (which comes with the tool when you buy it), you can test your monitor and fine-tune it to be able to accurately show you specific colors. Once it is calibrated, you can then create a "soft proof" on your screen by downloading a color profile or set of rules for the printer you are going to use. When you turn on that color profile in a graphics software program like Photoshop, the software makes a mock-up of what the printed file will look like on the chosen printing surface when the printer has applied its color translation rules. It's a complicated process, but essentially the software and color profile work together to show you a preview that is set exactly for the combination of printer, monitor, and surface you are working on.

NOW, FOR THE EASY SOLUTION:
Make a proof. The best way to see if you like the way the colors look is to order a swatch from Spoonflower and take a look. If that seems a little too unscientific, we have some tools to help.

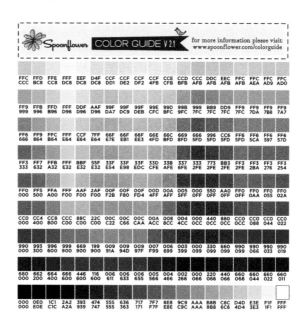

FIGURE 2 Our Color Guide features a selection of 171 colors chosen from our more extensive Color Map, which has more than 1,400 colors (page 50).

Spoonflower has created two different color resources, one more basic than the other. Our Color Guide (Figure 2) is a chart to help show colors as they actually print. It is an 8 x 8 inch (20 x 20 cm) swatch of Kona® Cotton with 171 color chips, along with their RGB hexadecimal (hex) codes. (For best results with our printers, we recommend using the RGB color mode throughout your design process, but we can also work with CMYK and LAB color modes.) The colors on it were carefully chosen because they print very close to what you see on many monitors. The codes can also be used in conjunction with a design program and with our Change Colors tool (page 53) to choose reliable color for your surfaces.

The Color Map (page 50) shows a much larger number of samples, with more than 1,400 color chips all marked with their hex codes. You can order the Color Map printed on 1 yard (.9 m) of any of our fabrics or 4 feet (122 cm) of wallpaper, and it will show you exactly what the colors look like when printed on the surface of your choice. You can find these tools at: www. spoonflower.com/ colorguide.

Spoonflower COLOR MAP V 2.1

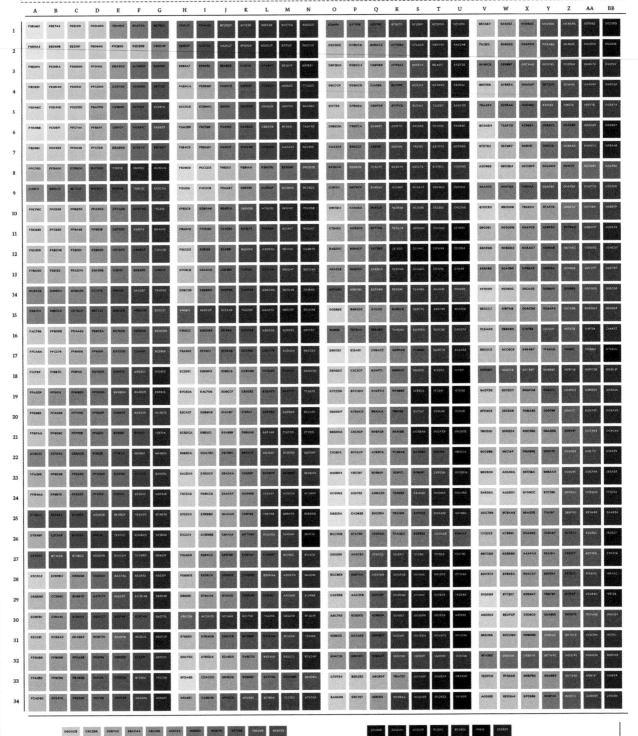

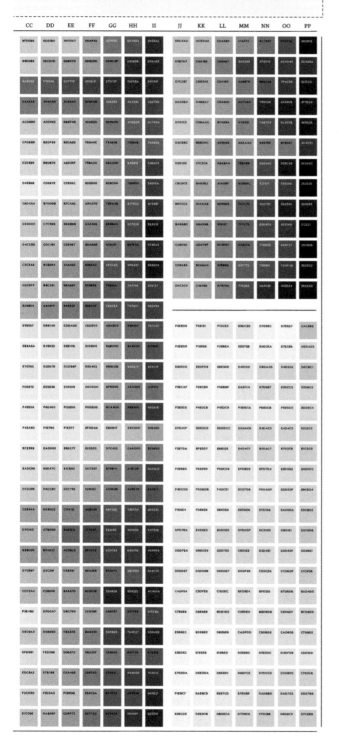

The **COLOR MAP** is a more advanced color tool than the Color Guide on page 49. Although the Color Map does not display *all* the colors that can be printed by the Spoonflower printers, it is a representative selection.

There are several ways you can use the Color Map:

MATCHING COLORS. The Color Map can help you coordinate your design to another object. Imagine you are making curtains for your bedroom. Compare the color chips on the Map to your bedspread or the paint color on the wall to find a color that matches. When you make a new fabric design and type in the hex code to set the color, you will know exactly what to expect.

CHOOSING COORDINATING COLORS. When deciding on a colorway—a collection of colors—for your design, choose a set of colors from the Color Map to jump-start the process. Then try the colors in your design. This is also a great resource to help when designing a collection of coordinating prints. If you use the same color code in different designs, you know the colors will match.

REVISING COLORS. Use the Color Map to help you revise colors in your design. If when you look at a test swatch you think a color in your design should be lighter or darker, find the original color chip on the Map and use that as a reference to help you choose the new color.

LEARN ABOUT COLOR

Using the Color Codes with Spoonflower's Color Map

Every graphics program will have a way for you to choose colors from a set of swatches or slider controls, or provide a place to type in a code for the color you want—a color palette. (See each of these in Figure 3.) To use the Spoonflower Color Map in conjunction with these tools, you just need to find the color you want on the Map and then type the 6-digit hex code (a4ddd1 at right) into the Color Palette tool in your design program. No matter how it shows up on your monitor, you will know exactly what it will look like when you print it out.

While it can be as simple as finding the color you like the best, colors are influenced by the qualities of the surface you print them on and how they relate to one another. So it's always a good idea to order a swatch to proof and confirm you like the color before you dive in to a large project, especially if you don't have the Color Map printed on the surface of your choice.

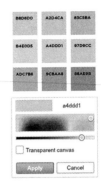

FIGURE 3 The color palette in your graphics program allows you to identify color by hex code or to choose colors from swatches or sliders.

Using Spoonflower's Collection Sampler

Spoonflower has a built-in feature to help you manage color and design decisions (Figure 4). If you are contemplating several colorways for a particular design (or several different designs), you can upload up to thirty variations and put them together into a Collection, then order a Sampler of all the designs printed together on one piece of fabric. To do this, go to your Design Library. Under "Views," select "All Designs." Click "Create a Collection," then give the new Collection a name and a description. Click "Create." Add designs to the Collection from the drop-down menu under each design's name.

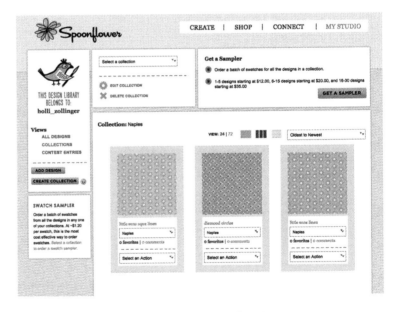

FIGURE 4 Test colors and designs in a Collection Sampler.

Using Spoonflower's Change Colors Tool

Spoonflower has a simple color manipulation feature built into the site called the Change Colors tool (Figure 5) that corresponds to the colors on the Color Guide (page 49). You can use it to switch colors in any design you have uploaded to Spoonflower, and you can keep both the new version of your design and the original.

First, the tool translates or simplifies the colors in your original and then displays a palette of color chips (up to twenty-four colors) that represent the colors in your design. It's easy

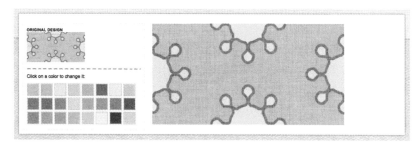

FIGURE 5 Our Change Colors tool lets you experiment with the colors in your design.

to use—simply click on the color you want to change, then click on the new color you want. The tool swaps out the new color for the old one every place it is present in the design.

The Change Colors tool can also help you create a colorway (a set of colors that make up your design) or develop additional colorways for an established design.

Fabric designers often create multiple colorways to experiment with color and contrast, and to explore how colors interact with one another. Here are examples from two Spoonflower designers.

HOLLI ZOLLINGER (holli_zollinger), Diamond Circles in light and aqua colorways

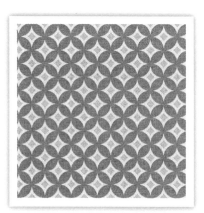

SHARON TURNER (scrummy), Triangles in tangerine and dusk colorways

WORKING WITH COLOR

Knowing how to put colors together and create surprising, striking, or pleasing combinations comes easily for some; for others, it takes practice and study. We asked one of Spoonflower's most popular designers, Kristi Holmes of Queensland, Australia, to tell us about her approach to color. Her textile designs often feature color palettes that are inspired by nature. Kristi is known as kristopherk on our site.

SPOONFLOWER: What role does color play in your work?

KRISTOPHERK: Color is a primary focus in all my design decisions. The physiology of color and our emotional response to color has always been a fascinating field of study for me. For example, have you ever asked yourself why food is often wrapped in red or yellow? It's probably no coincidence that the color red has been shown to increase your appetite and raise your pulse! Color influences our physiological state; it can help to excite, inspire, empower, warn, comfort, calm, or many other things.

SPOONFLOWER: What is your starting point for picking your colors?

KRISTOPHERK: I am drawn to monochromatic and analogous color schemes, using color palettes that connect me to the earth. These are colors that could be described as balanced, calming, peaceful, quiet, tranquil, and untroubled: color palettes designed not for eliciting a violently emotional response, but for grounding one in nature, in comfort, and in peace. It's colors like oatmeal, snow, toffee, cream, clay, charcoal, and smoke. Organic colors that work wonderfully together to create a calming and relaxing environment.

The designs Winter Meadow and Daisy Wash (see below) are good examples of that.

Sometimes I start a new collection with nothing more than a series of words—or a bubble map—to describe my emotional objective within the design. I will then select a series of colors to represent (replace) the words.

If you try this, remember that the balance and placement of each word/color within a design is vital; the mood in the bubble map will change when the dominance of each word/color changes.

My Winter Meadow and Daisy Wash designs reflect my preference for calming, peaceful color combinations.

This photo taken in Santorini provides inspiration for a new color palette.

SPOONFLOWER: How do you achieve color balance?

KRISTOPHERK: Often I squint my eyes (to ensure my vision is out of focus) to see if any colors or design elements "jump" out at me. Working this way helps to ensure that I have balance and harmony within each new design.

Another approach I like to take is to look directly to nature. Inspiration from the natural world is all around us. I like to document inspiring palettes whenever I can, simply by taking a photo to reference later on, or by recording the colors in a journal.

SPOONFLOWER: Any color tips for beginners?

KRISTOPHERK: Study the juxtaposition of colors in nature, at various times throughout the day.

For example, aqua-green leaves against a bold blue sky look quite different when viewed in the early morning light against a pale gray mist. You can see this in art: The series of artworks by Claude Monet featuring haystacks in the French countryside illustrates beautifully how changing light throughout the day changes colors—and in turn, influences our emotional response to the work.

One simple tip to remember is colors change not only with light, but also in relation to other colors around them. For example, the orange dots in the squares below are the same color, but they appear different depending on whether the square is aqua or yellow.

When selecting color palettes for designs and collections, remember not to select colors in isolation.

Your colors need to work together to achieve the feeling you're going for in the overall design. So, even what appears to be a simple color scheme of primary red and white can produce a different emotional response when it's a slightly warmer tone versus a slightly cooler tone.

And finally, a great place to start learning about color theory is a color wheel that outlines primary, secondary, and tertiary colors, warm colors versus cool colors, together with an explanation of different color schemes (such as monochromatic, analogous, and complementary).

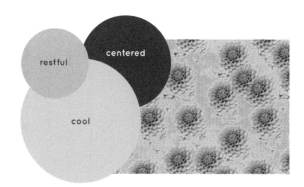

I created a bubble map to describe my emotional objective before I created Marie's Garden.

These two orange dots are the exact same color but appear different when placed in different colored squares.

OPPOSITE, LEFT COLUMN FROM TOP

I work in a variety of ways when deciding on colors, but rarely make my choices before I have designed. All my ideas and patterns are drawn in black and then scanned in and manipulated in Photoshop in this way. When I am happy with my work, I then take a step back and think about the theme and what feeling I want to convey with the colors I choose. Then I begin to make decisions.

—LINDSAY BUCK (slumbermonkey)

I collect nice color combinations when I see them on the street, in books, nature, and everywhere around me. It's like being a "creative sponge." I try to remember what I see or take a picture. When designing, I often have one color in mind (with this design it was a warm grey) as a starting point. Designing digitally gives me a lot of freedom to play and change colors 'til it just feels right: I love that!

—DEBORAH VAN DE LEIJGRAAF (bora)

My approach to color is simple: Let each color shine! I love pairing bold colors with neutral backgrounds for a fresh, contemporary feel. While my choices for color are mostly intuitive, I maintain a faithful relationship with what I call my "toolbox." This is an invaluable resource of colors, artwork, and photographs I've collected from all of my digital wanderings. Also, I've spent countless valuable hours devouring websites like Kuler and Colourlovers to discover and create new and innovative color combinations. Pairing this practice with an understanding of color theory and trending can help you create stronger designs.

—HOLLI ZOLLINGER (holli_zollinger)

OPPOSITE, CENTER COLUMN FROM TOP

My approach to color has never been scientific. I mostly rely on my instinct and past experience. Even though you may not have experience, you can find color inspiration everywhere. We see color combinations, as well as patterns, in everyday life. Carry a camera for when you come across beautiful or striking imagery. Note how color is used in advertising and merchandise packaging when thumbing through magazines or walking through a store. Visit art museums or artists' sites online. It helps in developing an eye for effective color combinations.

—MARIA FAITH GARCIA (mariafaithgarcia)

For a person who probably feels most comfortable wearing black and/or grey, it's funny to think that I actually love a *lot* of color in my textile designs. I gravitate towards designing with an even balance of cold and warm tones together. I like fresh, saturated, lively colors and tend to cringe at sad, drab tones that feel like they were left to languish in someone's attic.

—SAMARRA KHAJA (sammyk)

I take palette inspiration from everything. Vintage clothing, magazine pages, and flowers are my main sources, but I also get inspired by random visual moments in my life. For instance, sometimes I'm walking down the street and I see a pretty color combination formed by a hanging basket against a building wall. Once I see something inspirational, no matter how small or random it is, I log it in my brain for future use. I'm always keeping my designing eyes open, and my photographic memory is my most useful tool!

—GRACE NOEL (graceful)

OPPOSITE, RIGHT COLUMN FROM TOP

I find combining colors a little challenging. I always start with a single color and then add more one by one. Often I stop with just two or three colors because I'm content with the result. Lately I've been paying attention to the palettes of everyday life, such as the colors I see on old stamps, a row of books on a shelf, or piles of fruit in the grocery store. I also like to pair colors that feel dissonant, or don't exactly match. I recently crocheted a series of hats using three colors each and this was my formula: one bright color, one clashing medium hue, and one natural color. They came out really nice, so now I may try mixes like these on Spoonflower.

—ANDA CORRIE (anda)

Every designer has colors that they revisit and reuse. Think about the colors you enjoy having around you, and let your work be a natural expression of your own personal taste. So, I very much enjoy a tonal gray palette livened up with hot saturated colors, like red/orange/yellow/pink. I revisit this combination often because it pleases me! One tip I have for beginners: Try not to throw everything in. Overcomplicated color schemes can easily look muddy and dull. Keep it simple for sharp, striking, or subtle results.

—ALEX MORGAN (spellstone)

Picking colors does not come naturally to me; I never go with my first instinct. I always have a lot of designs drawn, just waiting for the right colors. When I see a color combination somewhere, in a picture or in something on the street, that I think fits with a design, I try it. For fabrics I design for other companies, I can't use an endless number of colors—the maximum is about eight per design. It can be a sport to make a design work with fewer then eight. Sometimes I go to colourlovers.com to create palettes or be inspired.

—NANCY KERS (verycherry)

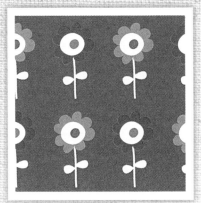

GET TO KNOW REPEATS

OPPOSITE We created a variety of repeats from a 3-inch (7.5 cm) flower shape we cut from construction paper, scanned, recolored, and uploaded to Spoonflower. After our designs were printed on linen-cotton canvas, we stretched the fabric over premade canvases from the hobby shop and stapled in back to create easy "artwork" to display.

When you paint a giant canvas or a big mural on a wall, you usually create one whole scene or abstract image that takes up the entire space. While it's true that you can do that with fabric, wallpaper, and paper, the real building blocks of surface design are repeats.

In the context of fabric and paper design, the word "repeat" refers to the element that makes up your design. To fill yards of fabric or paper, this element is duplicated over and over again—yes, you repeat your repeat! You can arrange your repeat (also called a block or tile) in grids of rows and columns.

Repeat Options

The Spoonflower site offers five different repeat options, each of which can be created with the click of a mouse once you have uploaded your artwork. If you want to test your eye on real fabric designs, take our quiz on page 202.

+ **BASIC.** The design is replicated in a regular grid of columns and rows, like tiles on a floor. You may see this option referred to as a block repeat or a square repeat elsewhere.

+ **HALF-DROP.** In this staggered layout, each vertical row of tiles is shifted a half-block from the one beside it.

+ **HALF-BRICK.** Another staggered option, the half-brick shifts the design block in horizontal rows, each row offset a half-block from the one below it.

+ **MIRROR.** A mirror repeat flips the design horizontally and vertically along its edges, so that each row and column is a mirror image of the one next to it.

+ **CENTER.** This option centers a single copy of your tile in the layout; it is the only layout we offer that is not based on a grid of repeated blocks.

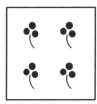

BASIC

HALF-DROP

HALF-BRICK

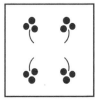

MIRROR

CENTER

Tile vs. Repeat

Some of the terms common to designing for surfaces are used as both nouns and verbs interchangeably. For example, the words "tile" and "repeat" are both used to describe a basic design element as well as the repetition of it. The phrases "tile a repeat" and "repeat a tile" both refer to filling a surface with continuous design.

Planning a Repeat

As you are planning a design, it's important to consider what size you want your repeat to be. Do you want to start with a tile that is 1 x 1 inch (2.5 x 2.5 cm) or 12 x 12 inches (30.5 x 30.5 cm)? It's helpful to think about your intended project; for example, see the Citrus Dish Towels on page 108. We knew we wanted small-scale repeats at a different size for each towel, and we knew that we wanted to fill the space with pattern. For quick reference, the limes are each 1 inch (2.5 cm) wide, while the larger oranges are 4 inches (10 cm) wide. There are certainly ways to resize and scale a repeat—some of which we use in this project—but it is helpful to have a concept from the beginning.

It is also important to understand how we tile the designs you upload. We repeat your design from the bottom left-hand corner; this is clearly shown in the preview in your Design Library.

Understanding Negative Space

Negative space is the area around and between the subject of an image and it can have a big impact on the look of a design. In the repeat patterns shown here, we varied the amount of negative space between each flower and also the color of the positive (flower) and negative space. When considering negative space, step back and look at your design from a distance. See if the negative space draws your eye in or disrupts the flow.

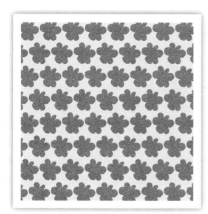

See for Yourself!

It's unbelievably easy to play around with different repeat options. Simply go to www.spoonflower.com and click "Create." Don't worry—you don't need to have anything designed, all you need is an image. You don't even need an account yet! After you click "Create," you'll be prompted to upload a file from your computer. Choose any image you want (such as a digital photograph) and click "Upload."

As soon it uploads, you will see a preview of your image in the basic repeat option, which is the default. You'll also see icons that represent the different types of layouts. If you click on each, you'll see how the layout changes to reflect the new selection. When you think you've got a handle on this idea, try taking our Repeat Quiz on page 202.

The preview screen is helpful in other ways, too. Notice how you can change the size of a repeat by clicking "Bigger" (if your file is more than 150 dpi) or "Smaller." You can also view your repeat as it would print on all of the surfaces; remember that each has a different width (page 33). You can even see a simulation of how wallpaper will look on the wall!

Seamless Repeats

On most fabric and wallpaper you can't easily see where one repeat ends and the next begins. That is because often designers intentionally make their repeats "seamless."

A seamless repeat is a way of designing a block to hide or disguise the repeat style you are using (it also hides the seams between the blocks). To make a design seamless, you need to make elements of it extend to the edges of the tile so that there is no obvious line, interruption, or empty space when the tiles are put next to one another. You still create the pattern using one of the layouts (basic, half-drop, or half-brick), but the design itself creates the illusion that there is no grid involved. Sneaky, right?

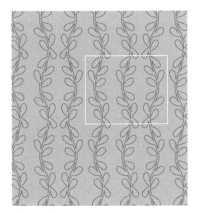

ABOVE The white box shows the repeat tile for this design. The elements of the design continue to the edges of the tile and match up when the tiles are placed side by side, disguising the edges of the repeat.

CREATING A SEAMLESS REPEAT

Here's an easy exercise to help you understand how a seamless repeat is made. All you need is a standard piece of copy paper, a pencil, and a pair of scissors. (In Chapter 8, we show you how to do the same thing digitally.)

Pick a random image to draw. Add different components to it but make sure that none of them touch the edge of the paper. Imagine that you made twenty photocopies of this sheet of paper and laid them out, according to one of the grid patterns we've learned. By repeating this block just as it is right now, it would be pretty easy to see where the edges of the image are because they are surrounded by blank space.

To turn this into a seamless repeat, you need to extend the image to fill most of the blank space. Here is an exercise technique to help you draw those parts of the image and make them match up easily.

1   Cut the image in half horizontally. Then, cut it in half vertically. Your lines don't have to be straight; in fact, cutting slightly wavy lines will help you match everything up later. Put them back in the original order.

2   Pick up the two pieces that are on the left and move them so they are on the right. Now pick up the two pieces that are on the bottom and move them so they are on the top. All of the outside edges of the original drawing should meet in the center and all of the wavy cut edges should be on the outside.

3   Carefully match up the four corners at the center and lightly tape the pieces together on the back so they don't move around. Fill in the empty space with more imagery (additional paisley elements were added here), drawing across the seams in the paper.

4   Carefully remove the tape and reassemble your drawing with all of the pieces in their original places. Now the elements of your drawing will continue over the edges of the block and connect seamlessly with the next block in the layout.

To preview your repeat, just make a few photocopies of the finished drawing and lay them out side-by-side in a grid to create a basic repeat pattern like the option we offer at Spoonflower. Once you have finished fine-tuning your drawing, you can scan it and use it to create your fabric, wrapping paper, or wallpaper. Or, you can use it as a guide if you want to create an all-digital design based on your artwork.

Step 1

Step 2

Step 3

Step 4

PART 2

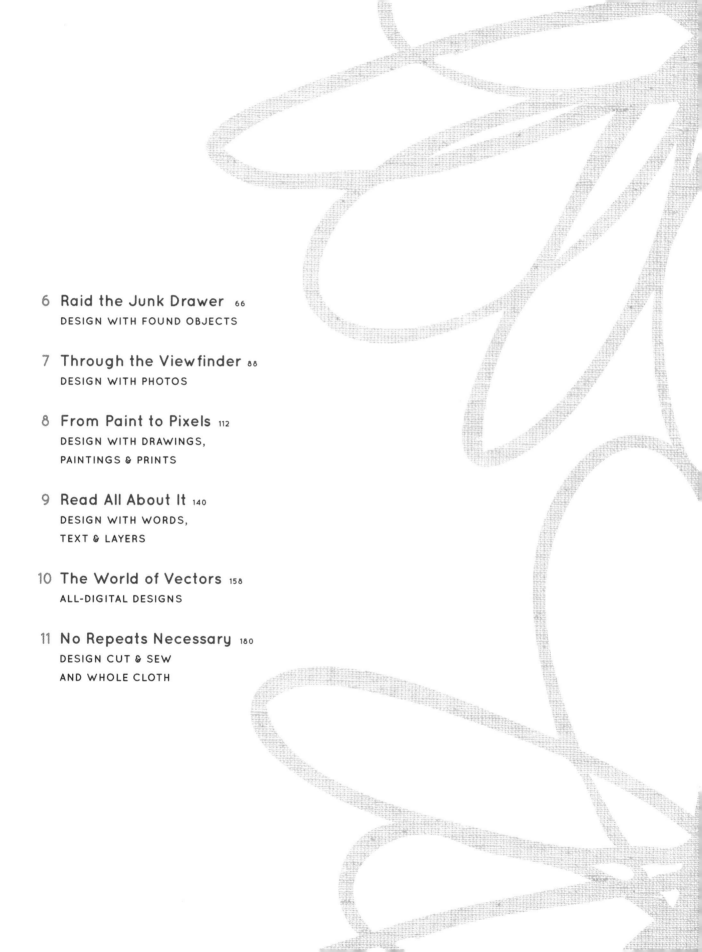

6

RAID THE JUNK DRAWER
Design with Found Objects

SKILLS LEARNED
IN THIS CHAPTER

+ Scanning

+ Sizing and Scaling

+ Basic Image Editing:
  Crop & Select tools

OPPOSITE Almost anything
you can put on a scanner
can form the basis of a
design, such as the postage
stamps used for this luggage
tag (page 72).

The easiest way to create a design is to start simple! A collection of objects (like feathers or stamps) and a scanner can be all you need to get started, without having to worry about your drawing skills. It's as easy as finding an object or group of objects that you like and scanning—presto! You are on your way to your first fabric design.

Spoonflower
2810 Meridian Parkway
Durham, NC 27713

How to Scan

Many people have experience with scanning, but we'll still start from the beginning in case you don't. First, place your original artwork or found objects on the scanner bed face down and close the cover. (Original artwork can mean many things, such as a painting or drawing, and found objects can include leaves, stamps, feathers, cut pieces of felt, or buttons that you put directly on the scanner.) Choose something that is relatively flat for best results.

TIP: If your image or object doesn't have a background that covers the scanner bed (a handful of buttons, for example), place a piece of paper on top of the objects before you close the cover. This ensures that you will capture a clean image with fewer shadows at the edges of your object.

Most scanners come with their own software. For example, the all-in-one desktop machines that print, copy, and scan have a specific program that opens automatically when the "Scan" button is pressed. You can also use a graphics program like Image Capture or Preview to scan.

Usually, your scanner will let you preview what you're scanning so you can make sure everything is placed where you want it, and then you can select the area of the image you want to scan. To do this, look for an option or button that says "Overview" or "Preview," and click it to see the preview. To select the part of your image you want to scan, click the image and drag to draw a box around your selection (Figure 1). When you make a selection in this way, you're cropping the part of the image that your scanner will capture. We give more information about using the Crop tool in an image editing program on page 71, but this is a quick and easy way to crop the image as you are scanning it.

Should I Scan It or Take a Picture?

You've created a piece of artwork on paper or canvas and you're ready to make a fabric design. Wouldn't it be easy to just take a photo of it? The advantage of a scanner is that your image is flat and parallel to the lens and the light is even across the whole image. With a camera, it's quite difficult to shoot perfectly parallel to your artwork and to get lighting that doesn't have variation and shadows. While you can correct most of these issues by editing later, doing all of that correction just adds extra time and effort before you can print your image.

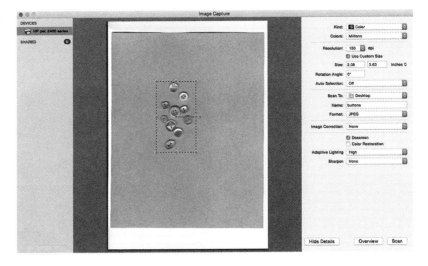

FIGURE 1 We placed buttons with colored paper on top of them on the scanner bed and began the scan. In Preview mode, we chose the part of the image we wanted to capture.

CHOOSING SIZE AND CALCULATING RESOLUTION

You will base the size and resolution of your scan on the size at which you want Spoonflower to print it. Remember that Spoonflower uses a resolution of 150 dpi to print, so all calculations should be based on that figure. Here is a simple formula to make this easy.

SCALING FORMULA

(SIZE OF FINAL ÷ SIZE OF ORIGINAL)
X RESOLUTION OF PRINTER =
RESOLUTION TO SET THE SCANNER

Work the part of the equation in parentheses first, then multiply that figure by the resolution of the printer to determine the resolution for the scanner. Here are a couple of examples of the formula in action.

OPTION 1: YOU WANT YOUR IMAGE THE SAME SIZE.

Let's say you have a piece of artwork that is 8 inches (20 cm) wide, and you want to print it at exactly the same size to make a potholder.

Drop the numbers into the Scaling Formula like this:

$$(8 \div 8) \text{ X } 150$$
$$1 \text{ X } 150 = 150 \text{ DPI}$$

This is a 1:1 ratio of finished design to artwork. Since 8 inches ÷ 8 inches is 1, and 1 x 150 dpi = 150 dpi, simply scan it at the same resolution that it will print—150 dpi. The shortcut for this option is: anytime you want to print your design at its full size, scan it at 150 dpi (Figure 2).

OPTION 2: YOU WANT YOUR IMAGE TO BE LARGER.

Now let's say you want to make a 16-inch (40.5 cm) dinner napkin from your 8-inch (20 cm) artwork. Here are the numbers in the formula:

$$(16 \div 8) \text{ X } 150$$
$$2 \text{ X } 150 = 300 \text{ DPI}$$

This is a 2:1 ratio of finished design to artwork. Instead of capturing 150 pixels in each inch, you need to capture 300 pixels in each inch (Figure 3). That will give you twice as many pixels, which is enough to fill a 16-inch space that is twice as large as your artwork. This retains the quality of the image.

This formula works equally well if you're defining the size of your image in pixels instead of inches, too, which is a common option in image-editing software.

FIGURE 2 Set your scanner to capture 150 dpi resolution if you want to print your design at actual size.

FIGURE 3 Set your scanner to capture 300 dpi resolution if you want to print your design at a 2:1 ratio, or double the size of the original.

SCAN AND SAVE

Now that you have done the math necessary to scan at the proper size, set the scanner to the proper resolution in the scanner setting dialog box. Look for a box labeled "Resolution" or "Quality" and type your resolution (dpi) in the box. Depending on your scanner software, it may only allow you to set it to standard defaults from a drop-down menu. Choose the number that is closest to—but larger than—what you want, and you will be able to edit later when you upload to Spoonflower. (Once you have uploaded your design, there are tools built into the site that will let you scale up or down to a certain degree.)

Next, choose the file type to save your image. For the projects in this book, .jpg is the best choice

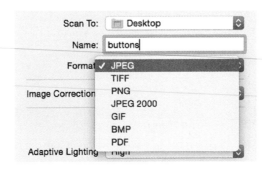

FIGURE 4 For the projects in this book, save your scanned images as .jpg files. This will be one of the choices in your drop-down menu.

(Figure 4). But there are many types of files and each one has advantages (see page 45 to review the file types Spoonflower accepts).

Finally, click the "Scan" button and save your file. (To keep your files organized, it may be helpful to save your designs in a designated folder, especially if you're just beginning to work with images.)

Refine Your Design

Once you have scanned your artwork, you may want to do a little editing before you're ready to upload and print your design. Open your .jpg file using your favorite graphics software. Here are a few of the basic tools you may want to use.

CROP TOOL

Cropping means trimming away the extra parts of an image that you don't want. For example, there might be stray marks (like the edges of the paper) that you would like to trim away—or you may decide to use only one section of a scanned and saved image. There are two ways you can crop an image: the Crop tool or the Marquee Select tool.

The Crop tool looks like two overlapping Ls. (Remember, as we explained earlier, each program has its own "different-yet-similar" version of tools with common functions.)

If you click somewhere on your image and then drag, the tool will draw a box showing the part of the image you would like to keep (Figure 5). You can adjust the area by clicking and dragging again, or by clicking and adjusting the corners of your previous selection. Once you have your area selected, you should click a button or checkbox marked "Apply" or "Okay" to confirm your crop. The part of the image outside of your selection area will be discarded.

MARQUEE SELECT TOOL

The Marquee Select tool works almost the same way as Crop. It looks like a box drawn with a dotted line.

Click and drag to draw a box around the part of the image you would like to select. Once you have selected an area with this tool, there are lots of things you can do with that selection, like copy and paste, move, rotate, and so on (we investigate those tasks more in later chapters). To crop the image using this tool, make your selection and then choose the menu item "Crop"—usually you can find it under the "Edit," "Image," or "Tools" menu (Figure 6). Don't forget to save the changes: Your program may or may not prompt you to save. Choose "Save As" to make a new copy and preserve your original image—you don't know when you might want to go back and use the original image again.

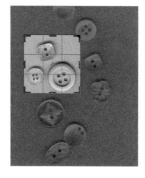

FIGURE 5 Use the Crop tool to select part of the image you want to use in your design.

FIGURE 6 With the Marquee Select tool you can crop and then manipulate a selected area of an image.

First Class Tag

JUDI KETTELER / CINCINNATI, OH

Judi Ketteler (known as ketteljm on Spoonflower) is a freelance writer; in fact, she is one of the writers of this book. She travels quite a bit for work, so her luggage gets a workout. Tired of the flimsy paper luggage tags airlines provide, she decided to make her own permanent tag. To create the background fabric, she scanned some vintage stamps; for the center section, she scanned her address.

designing the fabric

MATERIALS & TOOLS

TO DESIGN THE FABRIC

Collection of stamps (or other
  small objects like ticket
  stubs or playing cards)
2 x 4-inch (5 x 10 cm) piece of
  colored or patterned paper
Scanner
2 swatches of basic cotton,
  1 for the background and
  1 for the address, each
  8 x 8 inches (20 x 20 cm)

TO MAKE THE TAG

Printed fabric
8 x 8-inch (20 x 20 cm) piece
  of heavyweight interfacing
Scrap piece of paper, at least
  3½ x 5 inches (8.9 x 12 cm)
Grommet and grommet
  setting tool
Leather cord or your choice
  of material for hanging tag
Basic sewing tools (page 23)

1 Create a collage, scan, and upload.

Review the general scanning instructions on page 68. Arrange the stamps face down on the scanner bed in an 8-inch (20-cm) square. Overlap the edges of the stamps so there is no space showing in between them. Because you want to print the design at actual size, a 1:1 ratio, you will scan it at 150 dpi, which is the same resolution as the printer (page 69). Crop the image to trim away messy edges before you finish the scan (Figure 1). Save the file as a .jpg and upload to Spoonflower (page 18). Choose a basic repeat and print on a swatch of basic cotton; the design should fill the swatch.

2 Scan your address and upload.

Write your name and address on the piece of 2 x 4-inch (5 x 10 cm) paper and place it with your address face down on the scanner bed. Again, because you want to print your design at actual size, scan it at 150 dpi. Save the file as a .jpg and upload to Spoonflower (page 18). Choose a swatch of basic cotton fabric and a basic repeat (page 60). Repeating the design will yield multiple copies of the address, so you will have extra labels for other projects.

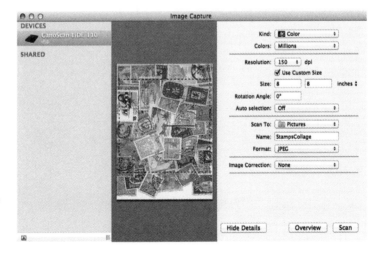

FIGURE 1 While in Preview mode, Judi cleaned up her stamp image by cropping away the edges.

Spoonflower
2810 Meridian Parkway
Durham, NC 27713

18

making the tag

3 Make the tag pattern.

Cut a 3½ x 5-inch (8.9 x 12 cm) piece of scrap paper. Fold it in half lengthwise. To make a rounded corner, trace around the edge of a drinking glass and then trim. Unfold the paper. This will be the pattern piece.

4 Interface and cut out.

Apply the heavyweight interfacing to the back of the stamp collage swatch following the manufacturer's instructions. Fold the interfaced fabric in half, pin the pattern to it, and cut two tag shapes. (If the interfacing is very heavy, you will have to cut the pieces out one at a time.)

5 Appliqué your address.

Cut out a fabric address label from the printed swatch. Pin the label to the center of one tag (on the printed side) and machine-stitch around all four edges using a zigzag stitch, pivoting at the corners.

6 Sandwich and stitch.

Place the two tags wrong sides together and pin. Using a buttonhole, overlock, or zigzag stitch on your machine, stitch around all sides. Be precise while sewing so that the stitching covers the raw edges.

7 Add the grommet.

Install the grommet to the rounded end of the luggage tag following the manufacturer's instructions. (Hint: If the grommet kit comes with a hole cutter, use the cutter to mark or score the fabric and then use a sharp pair of embroidery scissors to make the hole, as thick fabrics may be difficult to cut through.)

8 Add finishing touches.

Slip the leather cord through the grommet and tie to your travel bag as desired.

MORE IDEAS

+ Vintage stamps are fairly inexpensive and easy to come by (unless they are prized collectors' stamps). Look for them at flea markets or on eBay or Etsy. You can sometimes find them at scrapbooking and art supply stores.

+ Instead of stamps, try scanning anything else you like that will fit on your scanner bed: a map, your child's artwork, a handwritten list of your favorite destinations, ticket stubs, or foreign coins and bills.

+ For the address section of Judi's tag, Gina Sekelsky (lettergirl on Spoonflower) hand-lettered the address on a scrap of paper, which Judi scanned and printed. You can type your address (see tips for working with text on page 142), hand-write your address, or make it up ransom-note style with letters clipped from magazines.

+ To use a ribbon loop instead of a grommet to attach the tag, fold a 4-inch (10 cm) piece of sturdy ribbon in half and tuck the cut ends between the rounded ends of the two tag shapes before you stitch the sides.

SPOONFLOWER DESIGNERS RAID THE JUNK DRAWER

We're always amazed and inspired when we see the designs that Spoonflower users upload to our site. When we started looking around for designs based on scans of random objects, we found all sorts of interesting ideas. Here you can see designs made by scanning foreign currency; crocheted granny squares; a collage composed of a paper bag, masking tape, washers, and cutup colored paper; newspaper flowers; a tape measure; envelope liners. What else did we see? Peacock feathers, leaves, love letters, lace, magazine ads, cogs, shells, the list goes on and on. Now it's your turn. Raid your junk drawer, go for a walk, flip through a magazine, open your eyes. We can't wait to see what you dream up.

ABOVE, FROM TOP
HELEN SCOTT
(helen_scott)

MICHELLE RYAN
(nezumiworld)

ABOVE, FROM TOP
THERESA RIZZUTO
(trizzuto)

JANINE ZSCECH
(janinez)

ABOVE, FROM TOP
AMELIA REISING
(nightgarden)

SALLY HARMON
(boris_thumbkin)

Color Chip Lampshade

SARAH GIFFORD / MAPLEWOOD, NJ

Covering a lampshade with peel-and-stick wallpaper is an easy way to dress it up and personalize it. For this one Sarah Gifford (sarahgdesign on our site) gathered square paint chips at the hardware store, scanned them in a chevron pattern, and uploaded. We give instructions for making the chevron here, but you can arrange your paint chips in any pattern you like.

designing the decal

MATERIALS & TOOLS

TO DESIGN THE PAPER

An assortment of 4-inch (10 cm) paint color chips (about 8 different colors)

Masking tape

Scanner

Peel-and-stick wallpaper (size based on lampshade; see Step 3)

TO DECORATE THE LAMPSHADE

Printed wallpaper

Cylindrical lampshade made with smooth plain paper (see More Ideas on page 78 if you want to cover a different lampshade shape)

Basic sewing tools (page 23)

1 Create the chevron design.

To create a chevron pattern, stack your color chips one on top of the other, overlapping them as shown in Figure 1 so that you see about ½ inch (1.2 cm) of each color. Once you're satisfied with the arrangement, use a piece of masking tape on the wrong side to secure the chips.

2 Scan and crop your design.

Review the general scanning instructions on page 68. Place your paint chip design face down on the scanner, aligning so the "V" shapes are placed vertically. Because you want to print your design at actual size, scan it at 150 dpi. Crop the image so that your "V" is centered and there is no white space showing around your design, either cropping while you scan or working in your image editing program after you've saved the scan (also shown in Figure 1).

FIGURE 1 Paint chips arranged in a chevron pattern, scanned, cropped, and repeated.

3 **Save, upload, and print.**

Save the file as a .jpg and upload to Spoonflower. Choose a mirrored repeat (page 60) to automatically make a seamless repeat of this design.

4 **Determine size.**

Depending on the size of your lampshade, you will need to order a swatch or a roll of peel-and-stick wallpaper. To figure out what size to order, make a pattern out of a piece of newspaper and measure it to see if it fits on a swatch (24 x 12 inches / 61 x 30.5 cm) or a roll (24 x 144 inches / 61 cm x 366 cm).

To make the newspaper pattern, place the newspaper face down on a table. Using a pencil and ruler, draw a vertical line near the bottom left corner. Carefully line up the seam on the lampshade with the line you drew. Place the point of the pencil at the bottom edge of the lampshade and trace the bottom edge, running a pencil line along it as you slowly rotate the lampshade. Continue until you reach the lampshade seam again (the lampshade will have made a complete rotation) and make a small mark at both the top and bottom of the seam. Connect them with a straight line, using a ruler. Return the lampshade to the starting point and repeat the process to trace the top edge of the lampshade.

MORE IDEAS

+ We covered a cylindrical lampshade here. It's also easy to work with a cone-shaped lampshade. Be sure to make the newspaper pattern to figure out how much peel-and-stick paper you will need.

+ Use these instructions to cover any cylinder or cone-shaped object—plain terra cotta pots, canning jars, pen or pencil containers, etc. If there is no visible seam in your object to use as a guideline in Step 4, mark a spot with a piece of tape.

covering the lampshade

5 **Trace the lampshade shape onto the peel-and-stick paper.**

Following the instructions for creating the newspaper pattern in Step 4, trace cutting lines onto the back of the peel-and-stick paper.

6 **Cut out the wallpaper and apply.**

Cut out the wallpaper following the pencil lines. Peel a few inches (centimeters) of the backing paper from the wallpaper and line up the lampshade seam with one end of the wallpaper. Leaving the wallpaper face down on the table, slowly peel away the backing paper and roll and press the lampshade on to the adhesive. The peel-and-stick wallpaper is repositionable, so don't be afraid to adjust as you go. Trim away any extra wallpaper.

Another way to add interest to a simple design like this one is by adding a layer of texture. This is a preview of what we teach in Chapter 9 (page 140), but if you'd like, you can try it now. Once you have scanned, cropped, and saved your paint chip image, open it in your graphics program. Add a new transparent layer with a texture on top of the colored paint chip layer. Many graphics programs also allow you to adjust the texture layer, making it more subtle or more pronounced as you wish.

Or, if you prefer a lower-tech approach, simply place a very thin, almost translucent piece of paper on the scanner bed and then put the paint chips on top. Your scanned image will have a diffused texture. After you've cropped and saved either version of the image—low-tech or high-tech—upload to Spoonflower, print, and proceed as in the project instructions.

For the design shown above, we used paint chips in white and different shades of blue and applied a linen texture.

RAID THE JUNK DRAWER

Recipe Tea Towel

EMMA JEFFERY / HUNTINGTON BEACH, CA

Emma Jeffrey is a blogger and a member of the Fiskars Design Team. She made these tea towels from scans of recipes handwritten by her late grandmother. They were the subject of one of the most popular posts ever on the Spoonflower blog.

designing the fabric

MATERIALS & TOOLS

TO DESIGN THE FABRIC

6 x 4-inch (15 x 10 cm) piece
  of paper or index
  card with recipe (see Note)
Scanner
1 fat quarter of linen-cotton
  canvas, 27 x 18 inches
  (68.6 x 46 cm)

TO MAKE THE TOWEL

Printed fabric
4 inches (10 cm) of narrow
  ribbon, for hanging from
  corner
Pencil or fabric marker
Basic sewing tools (page 23)

Note: If the recipe or artwork that you want to scan isn't 6 x 4 inches (15 x 10 cm), use the Pixel Equation on page 42 and Scaling Formula on page 69 to help you adjust it to fit on a fat quarter.

1 **Scan your recipe.**

Review the basic scanning directions on page 68. Place the recipe face down on the scanner. If your text is vertical as in this project, place the long side of the rectangle horizontally when you scan so it is oriented properly to print (page 60).

To make the recipe fill a fat quarter of linen-cotton fabric that is 27 x 18 inches (68.6 x 46 cm), scale it up. The finished height of the design is 16 inches (40.5 cm). Use the Scaling Formula on page 69 to determine the resolution for the scanner:

16 INCHES ÷ 4 INCHES = 4

4 X 150 = 600 DPI

So scan at 600 dpi. This file will print at a finished size of 24 x 16 inches (61 x 40.5 cm).

2 **Save, upload, and print.**

Save the file as a .jpg and upload to Spoonflower (page 18). Choose a centered repeat (page 60) and print on a fat quarter of linen-cotton canvas, which is a great fabric for this project.

...................................196....

M...

.... 350° - 20 mins

Dr. to . . .

R. C. CLEGG
Road Transport Contractor

Golden Shorties

2oz Lard
20z Marg
4oz Sugar   } Melt in Pan
1 Teaspoon Syrup   too eight

1 Teaspoon Bi-carb
1 " Boiling water
4ozs Oats
4ozs Flour.

Stir flour + oats in melted
fat + sugar etc. Place small
teaspoons on greased baking
tin Bake 350° for 20 mins

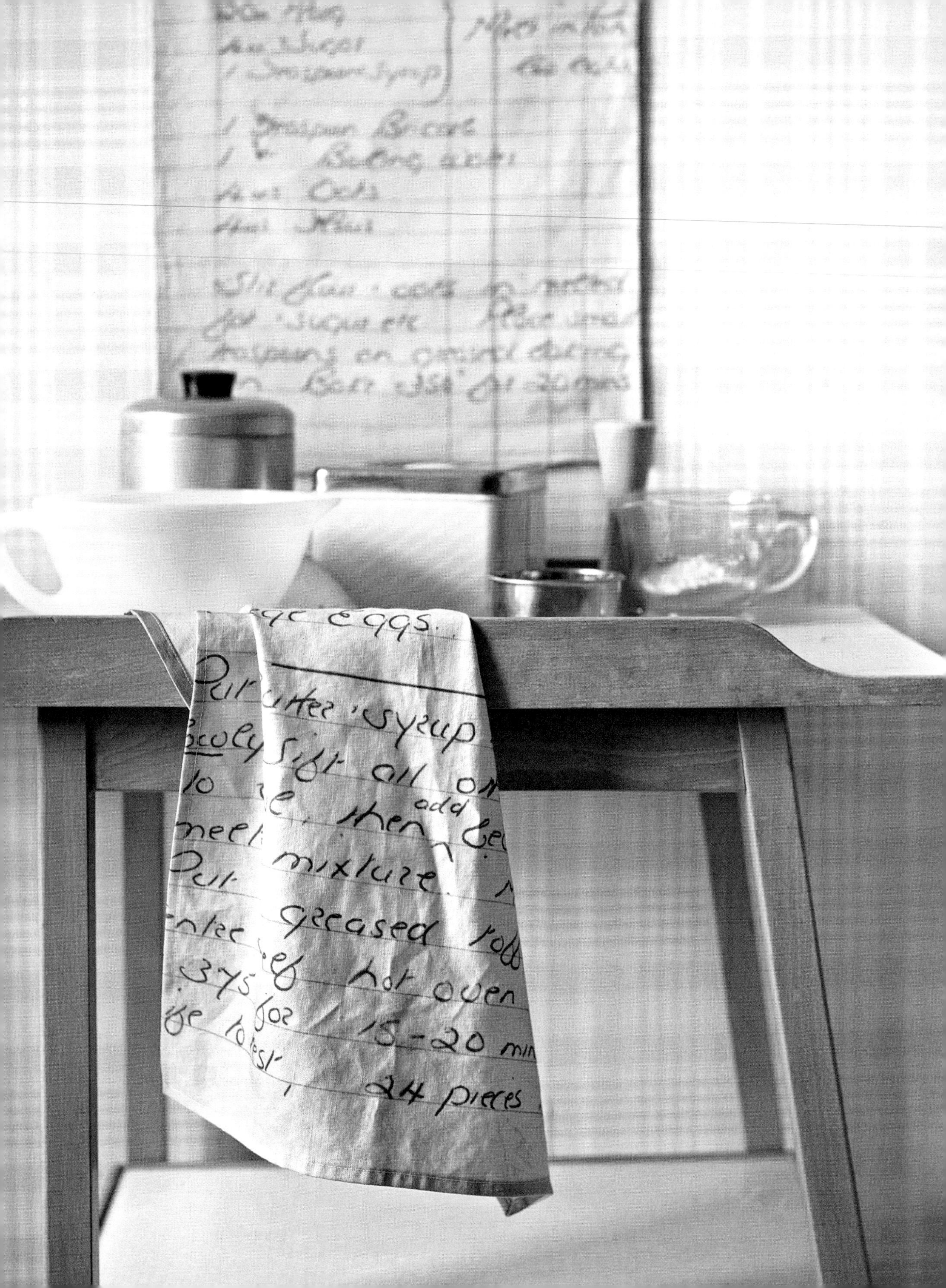
eggs.
mixture.
greased
hot oven
375 for
15-20 min
24 pieces

making the tea towel

3 Prepare your fabric.

Wash, dry, and press your fabric. Trim the fat quarter to 26 x 18 inches (66 x 46 cm) which includes a 1-inch (2.5 cm) seam allowance on each side.

4 Hem with mitered corners.

Turn under ½ inch (1.2 cm) on all sides and press. Turn under another ½ inch (1.2 cm) folding the raw edge of the fabric towards the inside. Press.

To create a neat mitered corner, open each corner. Draw a line through the innermost square formed by the folds as shown (Figure 1) and clip away this triangle (Figure 2). Fold the clipped edge under ⅜ inch (9.5 mm), then refold along the original pressed hemlines. Gently smooth the corner with your fingers and the folded edges should meet at a 45° angle. Pin in place.

5 Insert ribbon and stitch.

Trim the ends of the ribbon at a 45° angle. At one top corner, insert the ribbon ends under the folded hem so the ribbon slants diagonally across the corner. Pin in place. Stitch close to the inner folded edge of the hem on all sides, catching the ends of the ribbon inside the hem allowance as you stitch.

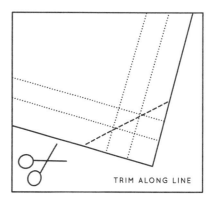

TRIM ALONG LINE

FIGURE 1 The light gray dotted lines indicate your fold lines. Cut where indicated by the black dashed line.

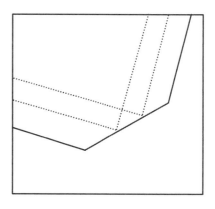

FIGURE 2 After trimming away the corner, fold the cut edge under ³⁄₈ inch (9.5 mm).

MORE IDEAS

+ Instead of a recipe card, try scanning a favorite quote or poem, a love note, or a message written by your child to create tea towels. Or, ask guests to sign an index card instead of a guest book at a wedding or baby shower, then scan and create tea towels for the newlyweds or new parents. As long as you use something that is the dimensions of an index card, you can follow the same instructions.

+ Add a sturdy piece of canvas as a backing and make placemats instead of tea towels. Just put right sides together, stitch, turn, and press.

+ Print the same design on peel-and-stick wallpaper, trim, and hang on your kitchen wall for instant art. Or use to line drawers.

Simple Flower Ornament

ANDA CORRIE / BERLIN, GERMANY

With a signature whimsical, hand-drawn style, Anda Corrie was one of Spoonflower's early users. She is a designer on Etsy's global brand design team in Berlin, and goes by the screen name anda on Spoonflower. She designed these ornaments when she was decorating her first child's nursery.

MATERIALS & TOOLS

TO DESIGN THE FABRIC

3 or 4 sheets of solid-colored paper in contrasting colors

White paper

Craft scissors

Black or brown felt-tip pen

Double-sided tape

Scanner

1 swatch of basic cotton, 8 x 8 inches (20 x 20 cm) (see Note)

TO MAKE THE HOOP ORNAMENTS

Printed fabric

5-inch (12 cm) wooden embroidery hoop

Embroidery floss in several complementary colors

Embroidery needle

Fabric fray stop or fabric glue

Basic sewing tools (page 23)

Small nail-less sawtooth picture hanger

TO MAKE THE PUFFY ORNAMENTS

Scrap of complementary fabric, about 6 inches (15 cm) square

Embroidery hoop

Embroidery floss in several complementary colors

A small amount of polyester stuffing

6 inches (15 cm) of decorative cord or narrow ribbon

Basic sewing tools (page 23)

Note: 1 swatch will make 1 ornament

designing the fabric

1 Cut out shapes and personalize.

From the colored paper, cut several 4-inch (10 cm) diameter circles and several 2½-inch (6 cm) diameter circles. Cut these as a freehand shape or trace a smooth circle around a plate or bowl, depending on the style you like. Draw initials, names, faces, or words with a felt-tip pen in the center of the smaller circles.

2 Assemble the design and scan.

Review the basic scanning directions on page 68. Use double-sided tape to place smaller circles on the centers of the larger circles. Lay the circles face down on the bed of a scanner, leaving at least 1½ inches (4 cm) between each circle for seam allowances. Depending on the size of the scanner, you should be able to fit 4 to 6 circles on the scanner bed.

Lay a white sheet of paper on top of everything, being careful not to disrupt the circle layout. Because you want to print your design at actual size, scan it at 150 dpi (page 69), a 1:1 ratio. Save the file as a .jpg and upload to Spoonflower (page 18). Choose basic cotton and a basic repeat layout (page 60) and print as much yardage as you need, depending on how many ornaments you want to make. A swatch will yield one finished ornament; however, if you plan to order only a swatch, you should crop your design (page 71) to 8 x 8 inches (20 x 20 cm) to be sure you print the full circle you like the best.

making the ornament

3 Mount the fabric in the hoop.
Cut out one circle, leaving at least 1 inch (2.5 cm) of extra fabric around the edges. Center it inside the wooden hoop. Arrange it so the hoop opening is at the center-top of the design, close the hoop, and tighten. Gently tug the fabric so it is taut along all sides and the surface is smooth.

4 Embroider to add details.
Use your favorite embroidery stitches to add detail and texture to a circle flower such as the one shown in the photo on page 84.

Here are some ideas to get you started:

+ Stitch straight lines from the outer edge of the larger circle to the outer edge of the small circle, radiating around it to make petals.

+ Use a few rows of running stitch just inside the edge of smaller circle to make seeds.

+ Use a backstitch to trace the initials or face in the center of flower and to create details like leaves.

5 Finish the ornament.
Once the embroidery is finished, retighten the fabric if it has loosened. Trim the fabric close to the back of the hoop and paint the edges with fray stop to finish. Glue the hanger to the back of the frame and hang.

6 Embroider to add details and texture.
Follow the directions through Step 3. Choose a circle and embroider as in Step 4. Remove the design from the hoop and press lightly to remove the creases left by the hoop.

7 Cut out a back.
Place the embellished flower face down on the right side of the complementary fabric. Pin through both layers and cut a second shape from this fabric to be the back of your ornament, using the front as a guide.

8 Stitch and stuff the ornament.
By either hand or machine, stitch around the perimeter of the flower about ½ inch (1.2 cm) from the edge. Start at the bottom of the flower and work around, leaving a 1-inch (2.5 cm) gap at the bottom to use for stuffing. Notch or clip around the edge and turn the ornament right side out. Stuff with polyester stuffing to the desired puffiness and hand-stitch the opening closed. Tie the thread in a secure knot.

9 Add a hanger.
Using a large needle and the cord, make a small stitch through the back of the ornament. Make a loop with the thread and tie the ends securely.

MORE IDEAS

+ Use a larger hoop. Since you can work with any sort of design element that fills your scanner bed, vary the size of your circles to create larger ornaments.

+ Use patterned paper to create the original artwork. Or use painted paper as Ellen Giggenbach did for her Flutter Baby Quilt on page 121. Also try shapes cut from a no-longer-used dictionary, newspaper, magazine, or map.

+ Instead of scanning a collage, scan and print a favorite drawing made by your child and frame it in an embroidery hoop (for the hoops at right, Judi Ketteler scanned her son Max's airplane pictures). See Chapter 8 for tips about working with original and hand-drawn art.

+ Make stickers by printing your design on peel-and-stick wallpaper. Simply cut around each shape and use to embellish a notebook cover, scrapbook pages, gift wrap, or whatever you desire.

7

THROUGH THE VIEWFINDER
Design with Photos

SKILLS LEARNED
IN THIS CHAPTER
+ Resizing Images

+ Using the Lasso &
  Move tools

OPPOSITE We turned an
Instagram vacation photo
into wall art by printing it
"poster" size, hemming, and
then nailing in place.

Photos are another easy way to get inspiration for a design—and they are plentiful! Whatever a camera can capture, you can translate into a cool surface design. Some photographic designs are very literal: The picture in its entirety becomes the design. But you can also crop out portions of photographs to use, or repeat elements from a photo to create a unique design.

Get yourself into creative mode by taking some time to look through the digital photos on your phone or your computer; try a stock photo site too, where you can purchase photos cheaply without having to pay a royalty fee each time you use them. Notice colors, shapes, and the play of light. Pay attention to elements that stick in your brain, and where your mind goes when you look at the image. Another great practice is to spend the day with your camera taking snapshots of anything that catches your eye. If you plan to use your photos for design later, it's best to set your camera to shoot at "highest quality" or "fine" so you capture a lot of pixels; we'll refer to these as "high-quality" photos in the project instructions.

Resizing a Photo

Chances are good that a photo coming straight from your camera is not going to be the right size for your design, so once you have determined the size you need, you will use the Resize or Image Size tool in your image-editing program to convert it. (Remember that we are using the term "resize" to reduce an image in size.) For many projects, you will need the image to be an exact size, and how you determine that is related to everything you learned about pixels, image size, and resolution in Chapter 3.

Resize is usually found as an item in the "Edit" or "Image" menu. Some programs call it Image Size (Figure 1). You can resize based on inches or pixels, in case one makes more sense to you in the context of your project.

When you choose the tool and the dialog box opens, fill in the blanks with the numbers you need. Look for a link icon or a check box that says something like "Keep Proportions" or "Keep Ratio." This will tell the program to keep the original shape or proportions of your image rather than distort it. In other words, if you started with a 4 x 6-inch (10 x 15 cm) rectangle and you want to make a smaller rectangle that keeps the same ratio, this option will adjust the width and height proportionally.

If the image needs to be a different shape than it started, you'll use both the Crop tool (page 71) and the Resize tool. For example, let's say the photo is a rectangle, but you want it to be a square so you can make a pillow cover, as in the Portrait Pillows project on page 101.

Crop it to a square shape first and then resize to the dimensions you need.

Also, remember this very important tip about pixels from Chapter 3—yes, technically you can make an image any size you want, but if you try to "add" pixels to make it larger, it will look pixellated and won't print clearly (page 43). So, if you look at your image file and see there are not enough pixels to do what you want to do, choose a new image—or take a new photo with the camera set to capture more pixels, if that's possible.

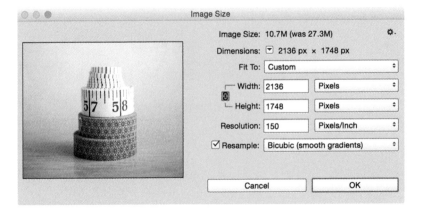

FIGURE 1 This is the Image Size tool in Photoshop. This is where you can enter the exact number of pixels you need for width and height.

Lasso Tool

With the Lasso tool you can cut an element from the background of a photo, like a single spool of thread (Figure 2), and use that element to create a repeating pattern (Figure 3). This tool looks like a loop of rope.

Click and drag the Lasso and you will see a dotted line appear where you have drawn. Make a closed loop by drawing all the way around the outside edge of the element you have selected.

Now you can copy and paste the element into a new blank canvas, where you can use it to create a repeating pattern or as desired.

Move Tool

The Move tool is used to move an element that you have selected. It looks like an arrow with compass points next to it.

Once you have made a selection with the Lasso tool, for example, switch to the Move tool by clicking it. This will let you click and move the element you have selected to a different place on the canvas.

Placing or Inserting a Photo

Sometimes you want to add an existing photo or image into the design you're working on. To add an image, use the "Place" or "Insert" command and choose the file you would like to add. Usually you find this command in the "File" menu.

FIGURE 2 Use the Lasso Select tool to trace around the outside edge of your selected shape.

FIGURE 3 We created a mirror repeat from the cropped part of the image shown at left.

Infinity Scarf

BECKA RAHN / MINNEAPOLIS, MN

Becka Rahn is a full-time artist and teacher, and a co-author of this book (she also designed the Squid Damask Shower Curtain on page 137, and the Stacked Skeins Skirt on page 193). She's been teaching textile design for years, and she always likes to show her students the very first design she uploaded to Spoonflower: a stripe pattern of little orange goldfish and bubbles. Becka (whose screen name is beckarahn) works from photographs a lot because she likes the organic texture they lend to a design. For this scarf, she worked with a close-up photo of a string of beads.

designing the fabric

MATERIALS & TOOLS

TO DESIGN THE FABRIC

A high-quality macro photo (page 95)
Basic photo-editing software
Flexible fabric tape measure
1 or 2 yards (.9 to 2 m) of silk crepe de chine, silky faille, or other lightweight fabric (we used silk crepe de chine)

TO MAKE THE SCARF

Printed fabric
Basic sewing tools (page 23)

1 Resize the image.

Review the general photo-editing instructions on pages 90–91. For this project, the image should fill the full width of the fabric. Since Spoonflower's different fabrics come in varying widths, choose the fabric to print on before resizing the image. We recommend a lightweight fabric with lots of drape.

Once again, our Pixel Equation (page 42) helps us determine how many pixels we need in the image. For example, if the fabric width is 42 inches (107 cm), you will need the width of the image to be:

42 INCHES X 150 PPI ▪ 6300 PIXELS

Remember, to prevent the image from distorting or squishing while being resized, choose the link icon or option that says "Constrain Proportions" or "Preserve Ratio" when resizing the image (Figure 1).

FIGURE 1 The little link icon connecting the words "Height" and "Width" shows us that the proportion of the image is locked. That keeps it from being distorted or squished while it is being resized.

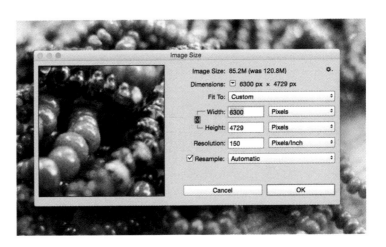

2 Choose the scarf size, upload, and print.

Use a flexible tape measure held in a loop to help decide the size that's right for your scarf; usually that's between 42 and 70 inches (107 and 177.8 cm). You can cut out the scarf parallel to the grain or perpendicular to the grain of the fabric. But ultimately, you need a piece that is 24 to 36 inches (61 to 91 cm) on the short side by your ideal length on the long side. The scarf shown here was cut to 24 x 42 inches (61 x 107 cm) before sewing.

Save your image. Upload the design to Spoonflower (page 18). You will need 1 to 2 yards (.9 to 2 m) of lightweight fabric to make the scarf, depending on the size you want. Choose a centered repeat if you order 1 yard (.9 m); choose a mirrored repeat if you order 2 yards (2 m).

making the scarf

3 Prepare the fabric.

Wash and dry the fabric. Press it to remove any wrinkles. Trim away the extra selvedge (the unprinted white edges) of fabric from the printed design and cut the rectangle to the size you determined in Step 2.

4 Match and sew.

Fold the fabric in half with right sides together and match the long sides of the rectangle. Pin.

Stitch, using a ¼-inch (6 mm) seam allowance. Your rectangle is now a tube. Reach inside the tube to the far end and begin to pull it through as if you were turning it inside out, but stop when the short ends are aligned; the right sides should be facing. Stitch around the short ends with a ¼-inch (6 mm) seam allowance, leaving a 2-inch (5 cm) opening for turning right side out.

5 Turn, press, and finish.

Turn the scarf right side out. Carefully press along the seamline at the long and short edges of the rectangles, taking care not to crease the edges of the tube. Stitch the opening closed by hand. You can wear your scarf as a single loop, or double it up for a cowl style, depending on the size.

MORE IDEAS

+ For macro photos for this project, look for anything that has great texture: weathered paint, stones, reflections in water, or shadows.

+ Other objects can make great designs for this project, not just photos. Scan a collection of autumn leaves, or feathers, or try ticket stubs or stamps like we did for the luggage tag on page 72.

+ Make the photo black and white. This works particularly well if you wear a lot of colors, because black and white makes a nice visual accent (and emphasizes the texture of the print). Look in your image-editing program for a filter or tool that will convert the photo to black and white before you save and upload to Spoonflower.

Becka's scarf design is created from a single macro shot—an extreme close-up—printed at a large scale. The best macro photos are high-resolution images with high contrast and one major design element that fills most of the image space.

HINTS FOR TAKING GREAT MACRO SHOTS

+ Set the camera to macro mode. This is usually indicated by a tulip-shaped icon on one of the menus or buttons on your camera. This helps the camera focus on objects that are close to the lens.

+ If the camera has interchangeable lenses, use a macro lens if you have one.

+ When framing the photo, choose an interesting area of the subject (i.e., the petals of a flower) and move in close enough to make that area fill the frame completely with no background showing.

+ Use a tripod or prop the camera to keep it steady and ensure a sharp photo.

+ Set your camera to a high-quality setting to capture the maximum number of pixels. Consult your camera manual to learn about settings.

THROUGH THE VIEWFINDER

Photo Panel Wall Art

Like the photos we used for the wall art on page 89 and the pillows on page 103, this photo was originally posted on Instagram. Photo panels are a great way to preserve all types of memories and to personalize your home.

designing the fabric

MATERIALS & TOOLS

TO DESIGN THE FABRIC
A high-quality photo
Basic photo-editing software
1 or 2 yards (.9 to 2 m) of basic cotton, sateen, or poplin (we used basic cotton)

TO MAKE THE PANEL
Printed fabric
Basic sewing tools (page 23)

1 Choose and resize a photo.

Review the general photo-editing instructions on page 90. Choose your photo and use the Resize tool to fit it on your fabric. The size of the file is based on the fabric you choose and the size of the finished panel you want to make. We used the Pixel Equation to do the calculations (page 42).

For example, 1 yard (.9 m) of basic cotton is 42 x 36 inches (107 x 91 cm). If you want your photo to fit the width of that fabric, then:

42 INCHES X 150 PPI = 6300 PIXELS

If you want your panel to be a different size, say 36 inches (91 cm) wide, you can resize the photo:

36 INCHES X 150 PPI = 5400 PIXELS

Depending on whether you have a landscape or portrait photo, you can also rotate the photo before you upload it to fit better on your chosen fabric. (To do so, look for something called Image Rotation, usually under the "Image" menu of your photo-editing program.) There are times where you can bend the "not enough pixels" rule and use a photo that's not-quite-high-enough resolution for a project like this, especially if you're printing on a highly textured fabric, but we recommend that you order a swatch first and make sure that the quality is what you want.

Keep in mind that when you order a swatch on Spoonflower, our system will automatically choose the bottom left corner of your design. You can see exactly what your swatch will look like in the preview. If there is another part of your design that you would like to check, you can use the Crop tool (page 71) to crop and save a section of the design without changing any of the

other settings. Upload this cropped section and print a swatch. This lets you choose a focal point of the design (like a face or the center of the flower) to make sure that the colors, quality, and sharpness are what you desire before you order the whole design.

2 Save and upload.

Save your image. Upload the design to Spoonflower (page 18) and choose a centered repeat (page 60). Remember that you will need 1 to 2 yards (.9 to 2 m) of fabric, depending on the finished size of your design.

finishing the wall panel

3 Trim and hem.

Trim your printed panel following the edge of the printed design. You may choose to leave your panel with raw edges, or you can hem using a couple of different techniques. To make a double folded hem, turn under ¼ inch (6 mm) and press. Turn under another ¼ inch (6 mm) and stitch close to the inner folded edge. To make a narrow rolled hem, see the instructions on page 178.

4 Hang your panel as desired.

We hammered small nails through our panel into the wall.

Choosing the Right Photo

Here are some tips for choosing a photo for this project:

+ To make a large photo panel like this one, your photo should be about 6000 pixels wide to fill 1 yard (.9 m) of fabric. Most newer digital cameras can take a photo this size with no problem, but this should be something to check as you are choosing a photo. Photos that are too small are probably going to look blurry or pixellated close up, although they might look clear from a distance. A little blur or pixellation can be nice if that is the aesthetic

you are seeking; if not, then it can be a disappointment so be sure to check carefully and consider swatching first if unsure.

+ Choose a photo with a lot of contrast. Contrast means areas of lights, mediums, and darks. Photos that are low contrast (all very bright or dark) can appear dull.

+ Look at the details. A tiny flaw when you look at a photo on your iPhone is going to look very

different when you print that photo as wide as a chair!

+ Think about the hem. You can choose to leave your panel with raw edges or hem them. Remember that a hem can take up about 1 inch (2.5 cm) around all the sides of your printed image, so make sure your hem doesn't hide something important.

Photographer **JENNY HALLENGREN** flew to the States from Sweden to take the pictures in this book. But before she got here she started sending us some of her own photos for printing on fabric. We were especially struck by this image of tree branches. First we thought about using it really large on a shower curtain, but ultimately we settled on these napkins.

To create this variation, first crop your photo (page 71) to a square shape.

When you are deciding how to crop your photo, keep in mind that ½ inch (1.2 cm) at each edge will be used for the hem, so anything on the very edge of the design will be not be seen. Also think about where the napkin will be folded when you place

your design. For these napkins, we planned to fold them in half lengthwise and then in thirds. So the bottom center section of the napkin features the photo. It's easy to print a test on regular paper and fold it like a napkin to check your photo placement.

Next, resize the photo to print at 17 x 17 inches (43 x 43 cm), which will give you a 16-inch (40.5 cm) finished napkin. Using the Pixel Equation (page 42), 17 inches x 150 ppi = 1550 pixels.

Save and upload your file to Spoonflower (page 18). You can fit one napkin on a fat quarter or choose a basic repeat (page 60) to fill 1 yard (.9 m) of fabric (making 4 to 6 napkins, depending on the fabric you choose). To hem, follow the instructions for the Citrus Dish Towels on page 108, omitting the ribbon hanger.

THROUGH THE VIEWFINDER

Portrait Pillows

These pillows are a great way to celebrate the people and places we love and want to be reminded of often. Make new ones each year and watch the family grow!

designing the fabric

MATERIALS & TOOLS

TO DESIGN THE FABRIC

One or more high-quality
  photos
Basic photo-editing software
1 yard (.9 m) of twill, faux suede,
  canvas, or sateen (we used
  twill) (see Note)

TO MAKE THE PILLOWS

Printed fabric
Backing fabric, ½ yard (.5 m)
  per pillow
Basic sewing tools (page 23)
Rotary cutter
Self-healing cutting mat
  and acrylic quilting ruler
Pillow form(s), either 16 x 16
  inches (40.5 x 40.5 cm) or
  16 x 20 inches (40.5 x 50 cm)
A small amount of polyfill or
  other stuffing (optional)

Note: If you prefer to make a single pillow, you can fit either the square or rectangular version on a fat quarter of twill. Resize the photos as described in Step 1, and create the canvas to be 29 x 18 inches (73.7 x 46 cm) / 4350 x 2700 pixels per Step 2. Choose a centered repeat per Step 3. Follow Steps 4–8 to make your pillow.

1 Measure your pillow, crop, and resize your photos.

Review the general photo-editing instructions on page 95. This project is based on pillow forms that are 16 x 16 inches (40.5 x 40.5 cm) or 16 x 20 inches (40.5 x 50 cm). To allow for trimming and a seam allowance, add 1 inch (2.5 cm) to each side, so your photos will need to be a total of 18 x 18 inches (46 x 46 cm) or 18 x 22 inches (46 x 56 cm) to fit one of the pillow forms made in this project.

For a square pillow, first crop your photo (page 71) to a square and then resize:

18 INCHES X 150 PPI = 2700 PIXELS

For a rectangular pillow, first crop your image to a 5:4 ratio rectangle. (This means that the length of the sides will have a relationship of 5 units wide to 4 units high. When you select the Crop tool, there is often a panel with options you can set to choose specific sizes or ratios to crop. To crop at a 5:4 ratio, look for a tool called "Constrain Proportions" or "Fixed Ratio" and choose 5:4.) After cropping, resize the image to 3300 x 2700 pixels and save the image. Review the Pixel Equation (page 42) if you need a refresher on calculating pixels.

2 Create a canvas and add photos.

Create a new canvas in your image-editing program that is 1 yard/36 inches (91 cm) of your chosen fabric width; for example, these pillows are made with twill so the canvas is 58 x 36 inches (147 x 91 cm) or 8700 x 5400 pixels. Place or insert each edited photo into the canvas; you should be able to fit 4 to 6 pillow covers on 1 yard (.9 m) of fabric, depending on the pillow size and the fabric width. The seam allowance is included in the design, so you can place them right next to each other.

3 Save and upload.

Save the file and upload it to Spoonflower (page 18). Choose a centered repeat (page 60).

making the pillows

4 Prepare your fabric.

Wash, dry, and press your printed and backing fabrics.

5 Trim and cut the backing fabric.

Since the pillow fronts were printed slightly oversized to allow for fabric shrinkage, trim them to 17 x 17 inches (43 x 43 cm) for a square pillow or 17 x 21 inches (43 x 53.3 cm) for a rectangular pillow, which is the finished size plus ½-inch (1.2 cm) seam allowance.

For the backing, you will need two rectangles of your backing fabric that are the same width as the pillow front. To calculate the height of each backing piece, divide the overall height in half and add 5 inches (12 cm). So, for the square pillow you need two rectangles 17 x 13½ inches (43 x 34.3 cm); for the rectangle pillow you need two rectangles 21 x 13½ inches (53.3 x 34.3 cm). Cut the appropriate pieces for the pillow(s) you are making.

6 Hem your backing pieces.

Turn under ½ inch (1.2 cm) on one long side of each rectangle of backing fabric. Press towards the wrong side of the fabric. Then fold another 1 inch (2.5 cm) to the inside so you have a deeper hem and press. Stitch close to the folded edge. Repeat for the second backing piece.

7 Assemble your pillow.

Lay your pillow front face up on a table in front of you. Place a backing piece with right side facing down, aligning the raw edges of the backing piece and pillow front along their top edges, hemmed edge towards the center. Place the second backing piece to align with the bottom edge of the pillow, with the hemmed edges of the backing pieces overlapping in the center. Pin.

8 Stitch, trim, and finish.

Stitch around all four sides of the pillow using a ½ inch (1.2 cm) seam allowance. Clip the corners, turn right side out, and press. Insert your pillow form. If your pillow corners look a little limp, you can add a little stuffing into the corners to plump them out.

Getting a Color Match

For the suede version of these pillows shown on the opposite page, we really wanted to make the back in the same fabric as the front of the pillows but in a solid color. So here's a teaser for Chapter 8: A really easy way to make a match is to use the Eyedropper and Paint Bucket tools (pages 114–115). Just choose a color from the pillow front and then make a solid-colored rectangle in the size you need to make the pillow back. Place this new rectangle into the blank canvas with your photos and print them all together.

DARCI MOYERS, a beloved Spoonflower employee for five years, snapped these photos while visiting Uganda. Turning the photos into pillows was a terrific way to preserve memories and continue to enjoy the scenery. Many programs, like Instagram or PicMonkey, will allow you to apply filters and effects to photos. For this project, Darci used Instagram filters Rise (adding glow) and Mayfair (adding brightness) to give the photos an intense, saturated quality—and printing on faux suede helped intensify the effect. Filters can be a great way to add another layer to your design, but of course they're not required. Follow the Portrait Pillows instructions to make these variations.

THROUGH THE VIEWFINDER

Doppelganger Dog Pillow

STEPHEN FRASER / CHAPEL HILL, NC

Although Stephen Fraser is the co-owner of Spoonflower, his wife, Kim, is still the one motivated to embark on ambitious domestic projects like making new curtains, wallpapering the bathroom with a swan design by Heather Ross, or sewing a new dress for one of their daughters using horse fabric—or Doctor Who–inspired fabric, depending on the daughter. Stephen (stephen_of_spoonflower on the site) is much more likely to try to create a plush dog pillow like this one, designed for Ruby, the first of the two rescue dogs that have come to live in their house. The best part? Unlike the real Ruby, the pillow version of her is actually allowed on the furniture.

designing the fabric

MATERIALS & TOOLS

TO DESIGN THE FABRIC

A high-quality pet photo (see page 106 for more information about shooting a pet photo)

Basic photo-editing software

1 fat quarter of linen-cotton canvas, 27 x 18 inches (68.6 x 46 cm) or the fabric of your choice; other good options include faux suede, twill, or sateen

TO MAKE THE PILLOW

Printed fabric

1 fat quarter of a complementary fabric, 27 x 18 inches (68.6 x 46 cm); see "Getting a Color Match" on page 102 if you prefer to print your own fabric

Washable fabric-marking pen or chalk

Polyfill or other stuffing

Basic sewing tools (page 23)

1 Choose a photo and size it.

Review the general photo-editing instructions on page 90. Choose a photo of a pet that is bright and clear with nothing in front of him or her. Use the Crop tool (page 71) to crop close to all sides of the image, cropping away any extra background. The longest side of the image should be about 20 inches (50 cm), so it can fit on a fat quarter. According to our Pixel Equation (page 42):

20 INCHES X 150 PPI = 3000 PIXELS

Resize to make the longest dimension of the image 3000 pixels (Figure 1). Be sure to click the "Keep Proportions" or Lock icon to make sure you don't squish the image.

FIGURE 1 To fit the image on a linen-cotton fat quarter, we determined that the longest side needed to measure 20 inches (50 cm) / 3000 pixels.

THROUGH THE VIEWFINDER

2 Select your pet.

Use the Lasso tool (page 91) to carefully select your pet by drawing a selection line around the outside edge. Then copy the selection using the Copy function from the Edit menu (Figure 2).

3 Create a new canvas and paste.

Create a new file that is 27 x 18 inches (68.6 x 46 cm) / 4050 x 2700 pixels at 150 ppi (Figure 3). This is the size of a fat quarter of our linen-cotton fabric.

Paste your copied pet image into the new canvas. With the image selected, click and drag it with the Move tool (page 91) to center it. Depending on the shape of your pet, you may need to rotate the image 90° to fit it on the fat quarter; remember that your image will print across the 27-inch (68.6 cm) width (page 107). Look for an option to "Rotate" in the "Edit" or "Image" menu or a Rotate tool that looks like a circular arrow.

Note: Stephen decided to have a little fun with Ruby's photo and used an adjustment in Photoshop called "Posterize" to soften her colors and then experimented with other filters until he created the effect he liked. You can use effects to manipulate your pet's photo too, or just use the photo as it is.

4 Save, upload, and print.

Save the image. Upload it to Spoonflower (page 18), choose a fat quarter of the design on linen-cotton or the fabric of your choice and a centered repeat (page 60).

FIGURE 2 Stephen outlined Ruby with the Lasso tool then copied the selected area.

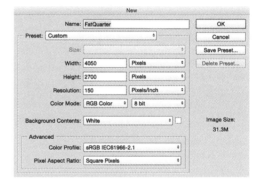

FIGURE 3 Next Stephen pasted the copy into a new canvas sized for a fat quarter.

Here are a few tips to help you shoot a great photo of your pet to use in this project.

+ Choose a photo that shows your entire pet with nothing overlapping or obscuring him or her.

+ Make sure the background is pretty clean. If you can get your pet to sit in front of a blank wall or on the sidewalk, it will be easier to crop him or her out of the image to make the pillow design.

+ It helps to have good contrast (page 98) in your photo. If you have a dark-colored pet, try to shoot on a light background; do the opposite if you have a light-colored pet. Taking a photo with lots of light or on a bright day will help you see details better when your photo is printed. You can also adjust the brightness and contrast of the photo after you take it.

+ Take several different views of your pet to be sure you capture his or her endearing features, such as big, perky ears; a short, curly tail; or a long, handsome nose.

making the pillow

5 Cut out your pet's shape.

Use a ruler and the fabric-marking pen to draw a seam allowance line ½ inch (1.2 cm) around the outside of the image. Trim away the extra fabric, following the seam allowance line. Place the pet fabric piece and the backing fabric right sides together. Pin the two pieces together and trim the backing fabric to match the edges of the printed piece.

6 Stitch and stuff.

Stitch around the edge of pillow using a ½-inch (1.2 cm) seam allowance, leaving a gap of about 4 inches (10 cm) in the seam at the bottom or side for stuffing. Clip the seam allowance around the curves and corners. Turn the pillow right side out and stuff it to the desired firmness. Slipstitch the opening closed.

Citrus Dish Towels

Making these cheerful dish towels is quick and easy using photos taken with any basic digital camera. Take a look in your fridge and at your local market and you're likely to find lemons, limes, grapefruits, and other fun, photogenic food, such as kiwis, star fruit, or heirloom tomatoes and potatoes in colorful shades. If you want to change to a non-food theme, photograph other items that are fairly flat, such as buttons, coins, or game pieces, for best results.

designing the fabric

MATERIALS & TOOLS

TO DESIGN THE FABRIC

A high-quality photograph of fruit slices (or similar small flat objects) (see Note)

Basic photo-editing software

1 fat quarter of linen-cotton canvas per towel, 27 x 18 inches (68.6 cm x 46 cm)

TO MAKE THE TOWELS

Printed fabric

4 inches (10 cm) of narrow ribbon per towel, approximately ½ to ¾ inches (1.2 to 1.9 cm) wide

Basic sewing tools (page 23)

1 Crop and resize the photo.

Review the general photo-editing instructions on page 90. Use the Crop tool to crop close to all sides of the object. Don't worry if you have extra "junk" or shadows in the background of your photo—these will be removed in Step 2.

For this project, we made several repeat patterns in different sizes. The limes, for example are about 1 inch (2.5 cm) wide when printed, or 1 inch x 150 pixels per inch = 150 pixels. For the largest orange, we resized the photo to 4 inches x 150 pixels per inch = 600 pixels. (See "Putting Multiple Images Together" on page 111 for more about creating the "Fruit Salad" towel in the center.)

Choose a size for your repeat and then resize the image (page 90) so that the longest dimension of the image is the size you calculated. Be sure to click the "Keep Proportions" or Lock icon to make sure you don't squish the image.

2 Select your fruit.

Use the Lasso tool (page 91) to carefully select the object by drawing a selection line around the outside edge. Take your time to get a nice smooth selection, then copy it using Copy from the "Edit" menu. By cutting out the fruit you can remove any imperfections in the background.

Note: Place the fruit slice or other object on a white plate or cutting board and take the photo from above. To avoid shadows, shoot your photo where there is soft, diffuse light from multiple sources.

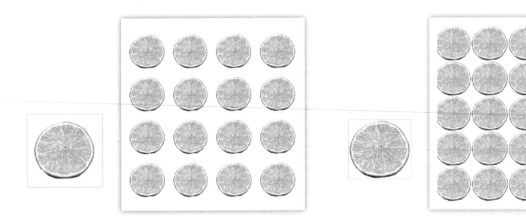

FIGURE 1 The amount of space you leave around your object in your original image (see small boxes above) will affect how the design will look in repeat (see large boxes above). The design on the right is clearly denser than the design on the left.

3 Create a new canvas and paste.

Create a new canvas (page 106) that is slightly larger than your object; this allows for some white space around the image. (For example, for the 150-pixel-wide image of the lime, we made a canvas that was 200 x 200 pixels.) Paste your object into this new canvas. With the image selected, use the Move tool (page 91) to click and drag it to center it in the canvas. See "Understanding Negative Space" on page 61 and refer to Figure 1 to help you choose the size of your canvas.

4 Save, upload, and print.

Save the image. Upload it to Spoonflower (page 18) and choose your favorite repeat style (see page 60 for a refresher). You will need a fat quarter of fabric for each dish towel you decide to make.

making the dish towel

5 Prepare your fabric.

Wash, dry, and press your fabric. Trim away the selvedges (unprinted edges).

6 Hem and finish.

To create a neat mitered corner as you hem and then add a ribbon hanger, follow the directions used in Steps 4 and 5 of the Recipe Tea Towel (page 80).

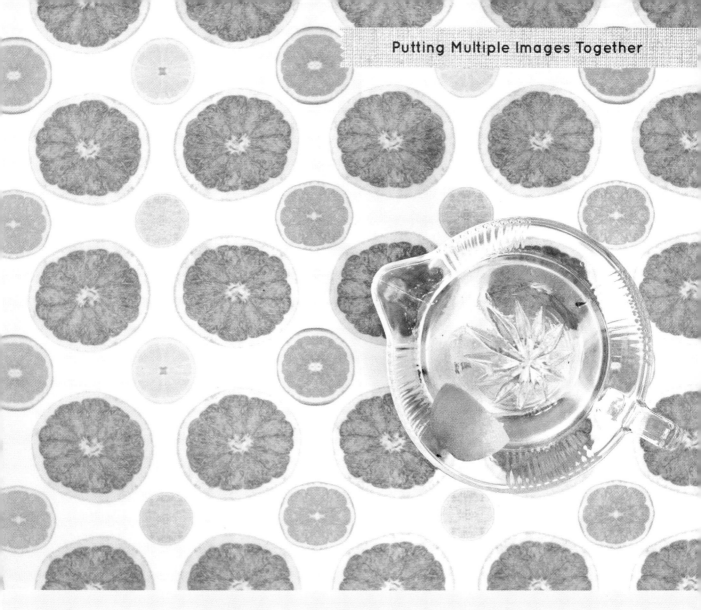

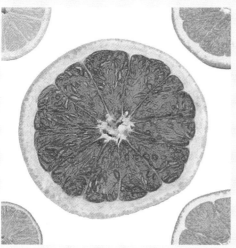

To make the "Fruit Salad" version of this design that combines several images, follow the same steps to resize each image and cut each out from the background with the Lasso tool as in Step 2. Then create a new blank canvas that is about twice the size of your largest image; for example, if your largest image is 150 x 150 pixels, make a new blank canvas that is 300 x 300 pixels, and add the images as in Step 3. For this design, we placed the grapefruit in the center and then used the Move tool (page 91) to put oranges, lemons, and limes in the corners of the canvas as shown, having about one-quarter of the image in the design and leaving the rest of each image to extend off the edges of the canvas. (You may need to know a little bit about Layers to do this, depending on your graphics program; check out page 142 for the basics.) Save and upload your design and then choose a mirrored repeat. The mirror effect will make anything at the edges of your design look like it matches up, creating an easy seamless repeat; in this case, because the original image is a round object, it makes your fruit look "whole" again.

THROUGH THE VIEWFINDER

FROM PAINT TO PIXELS
Design with Drawings, Paintings & Prints

OPPOSITE We used a floral
coloring book design by
Suzanne Dye for this scarf;
we also used it to create
the wallpaper on page 125.

One of the things we see at Spoonflower nearly every day is that the ephemera of life makes some of the most interesting and poignant designs. The drawings your kids create, the doodles and sketches that come from your imagination, the vintage postcard that inspires you to grab your paintbrush and create—it's all teeming with design possibility!

Creating a design from an original piece of art on paper is a fantastic way to start a project. After you've made your art, the next step is to scan it and make it digital as you learned in Chapter 6. Once you have a design on your computer screen in front of you, there are some easy enhancements and fixes you can make in your graphics program before printing it. For example, you can touch up some areas in your artwork, like removing stray pencil lines or cleaning up a wobbly or smudged area. You can also experiment with changing colors. Let's explore some of the tools that will help you.

Eyedropper Tool

These two tools are pretty easy to recognize: The Eyedropper tool looks like an eyedropper and the Paintbrush tool looks just like a paintbrush. You can use these two tools together to touch up a scanned image.

The Eyedropper allows you to select a color you want from your design and "copy" it so that you can put it somewhere else in the design. After you've opened your image in your graphics program, click with the Eyedropper to choose the exact color from the spot that you click. See which color you've selected by finding the color palette in your graphics program, as shown in Figure 1. It usually looks like a set of colored rectangles or a painter's palette, and the largest or most prominent rectangle shows the color you have selected.

Paintbrush Tool

To remove a stray mark from the background of the image, click with the Eyedropper and select the color of the background. Switch to the Paintbrush tool and use the brush to paint with the color you have selected. Paint over any lines or smudges that you want to make disappear. You can tweak your design in this same way: Select a different paint color and add in new lines or shapes to the artwork. Look for a menu item or palette (a set of tools or functions) that is labeled "Brushes." You'll find options for changing the size, shape, and edges of the brush—yielding many different effects that you can use to your advantage (Figure 2). Many of the other tools featured in this book also have palettes or panels that offer additional functionality.

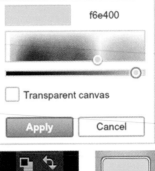

FIGURE 1 Here are three examples of color palette tools from three graphics programs (clockwise from top): Photoshop, Pixlr, and PicMonkey. They look a little different, but all function in the same way. In these screenshots we show what you'll see when you choose a color with the Eyedropper tool.

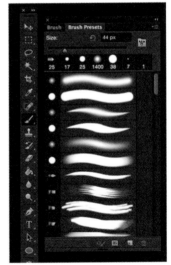

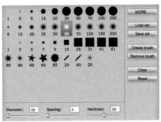

FIGURE 2 By selecting different brushes, you can achieve a variety of effects.

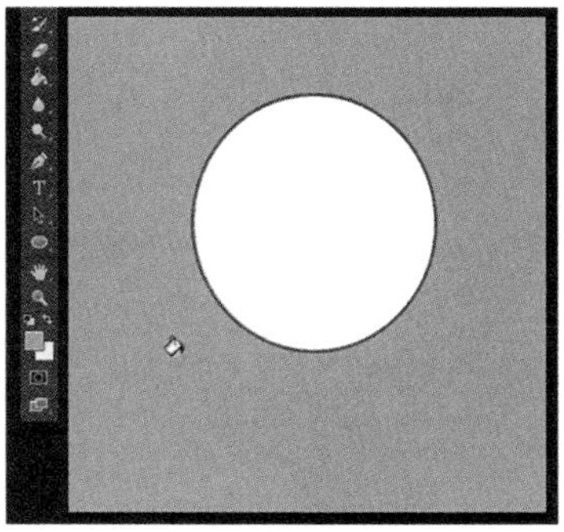

FIGURE 3 When you use the Paint Bucket tool, the paint flows around any objects already in place. To select an object to fill, you first need to define it with the Lasso or Marquee Select tool.

Paint Bucket Tool

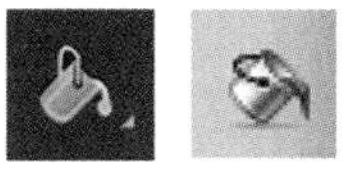

The Paint Bucket tool looks like a bucket of paint that is about to tip over—that icon tells you a lot about how the tool works!

Use the Paint Bucket when you want to fill in a large area of color, like the background for an image. Choose a color from the palette in your graphics program, and when you click on the image with the Paint Bucket, it "spills" the paint and flows into the image. If you have a blank page and click, it will fill the entire space. However, if you already have objects on the page, the paint will flow around them (Figure 3). To fill a complicated shape, you might need to click to fill each area one by one; to fill a specific area, use the Lasso or Marquee Select tool to define that area and then use the Paint Bucket tool to fill it with color.

Magic Wand Tool

This tool looks like a wand with a sparkle or star on top of it.

You already know how to select parts of an image using the Lasso and Marquee Select tools (page 71). The Magic Wand tool helps select parts of the image not based on a line that you trace, but on the color that you click. When you click on the image with the Magic Wand, the tool selects everything that is the same color as the point you clicked. Usually, the tool has options you can set to fine-tune what it is selecting. "Contiguous" means that when you click a color, you select all of that color that is touching the spot you clicked, not everything on the entire image. "Tolerance" tells the tool how picky to be about finding exactly the color you clicked. A high tolerance setting means, "Pick this red and any other shade of red that is pretty close to this," while a low tolerance setting means, "Be exact."

Daphne's Party Napkins

SARAH GIFFORD / MAPLEWOOD, NJ

Sarah Gifford is the graphic designer who designed this book. When she asked her daughter Daphne if she wanted to draw some pictures for party napkins, Daphne was quick to agree, and then big sister Della and friend Ali decided to join in. Each girl drew her pictures using black markers on an ordinary piece of white copy paper. Sarah scanned five of them (birthday cake, unicorn, mermaid, dog in a party hat, and pig in a party hat), played around with repeats and colors (with Daphne by her side for approvals), and then uploaded and printed them. The girls are thrilled, of course.

designing the fabric

MATERIALS & TOOLS

TO DESIGN THE FABRIC

A piece of artwork, ideally about 2 to 3 inches (5 to 7.5 cm) square

Scanner

1 yard (.9 m) of basic cotton, cotton, poplin, or sateen (we used basic cotton)

TO MAKE THE NAPKINS

Printed fabric

Rotary cutter, self-healing cutting mat, and acrylic quilting ruler

Basic sewing tools (optional— page 23)

1 Scan the artwork.

Choose the drawings to use for your napkin designs. Artwork that is between 2 and 3 inches (5 and 7.5 cm) square is ideal because of the small scale of this project.

We wanted the finished design to be the same size as the original drawings, so we scanned each drawing at 150 dpi (see the Scaling Formula on page 69 if needed). Scan and save each drawing you want to use for the designs; refer to page 68 for more information on scanning.

2 Clean up, crop, and refine.

Review the basic information on refining your artwork (pages 114–115). Open each scanned file in your image-editing program and use the Paintbrush and Eyedropper tools to clean up any stray marks or smudges. Then crop close to the edges of the artwork. If you want to change the color of the drawings, as Sarah did, use the Magic Wand and Paint Bucket tools to play with the artwork as desired (page 115). (To easily pick the entire drawing with the Magic Wand tool, be sure that "Contiguous" is not checked.) You can change the background colors separately, using the same set of tools.

3 Save and upload.

Save the image. Upload it to Spoonflower (page 18) and choose your favorite repeat style (page 60)—we used different repeat styles for the different drawings shown here. For example, the cake design is a half-brick layout. Print onto 1 yard (.9 m) of basic cotton, poplin, or sateen.

making the napkins

4 Prepare the fabric and trim.

Wash, dry, and press the fabric. Using the rotary cutter, ruler, and mat, trim the napkins to size. If you prefer cocktail napkins, trim to 12 x 12 inches (30.5 by 30.5 cm); for dinner napkins, as shown in the collection in this photo, trim to 16 x 16 inches (40.5 x 40.5 cm). From 1 yard (.9 m) of fabric, you will get about 9 cocktail napkins or about 4 dinner napkins.

5 Finish the napkins (optional).

For this project, we chose to keep the napkins very casual and leave them unhemmed. Alternatively, you could cut the edges with pinking shears, which will help prevent them from raveling when washed, or you can hem the edges following the instructions for the Recipe Tea Towel (page 80) or the Pet Silhouette Hankies (page 176).

MORE IDEAS

+ To make napkins in a variety of colors, you can print each design on a separate fat quarter; follow the basic instructions on page 116 to create your design, upload, and choose a repeat. You can get one 16 x 16-inch (40.5 x 40.5 cm) napkin per fat quarter.

+ If you have more advanced design skills already, you can create 16 x 16-inch (40.5 x 40.5 cm) designs in your graphics program and insert them into a larger canvas before you upload to Spoonflower, which can give you a little more versatility. In Spoonflower, print a yard of fabric; cut between the 16-inch (40.5 cm) repeats to make individual napkins.

+ For a fun option like the dog-in-a-party-hat design shown here, cut out your napkins on the bias (page 30). It does result in some leftover fabric, but that means you'll have some to repurpose into other projects (make fanciful napkin rings to use with your solid-color napkins, for example). You can also create a diagonal pattern in your graphics program by selecting and rotating your image 45°.

Flutter Baby Quilt

ELLEN GIGGENBACH / WELLINGTON, NEW ZEALAND

Ellen Giggenbach (ellengiggenbach on Spoonflower) hails from New Zealand (by way of Bavaria) and studied graphic design in Vienna. She is a freelance designer who creates art for textiles, books, greeting cards, stationery, home goods, and other products; she also has her own Etsy shop. For the fabric that she created for this baby quilt, she handpainted paper in different colors; cut out shapes and layered them to create a butterfly and flower scene; then scanned her artwork and scaled it up so it would fit on exactly 1 yard (.9 m) of fabric.

MATERIALS & TOOLS

TO DESIGN THE FABRIC

Original artwork

Scanner

1 yard (.9 m) of basic cotton

TO MAKE THE QUILT

Printed fabric

40 x 48 inches (101.6 x 122 cm) of cotton batting (we recommend Warm & Natural by Warm Company for its weight and durability)

1¼ yards (1.2 m) of coordinating fabric for backing (see Note)

½ yard (.5 m) coordinating fabric for binding (see Note)

Masking tape

Rotary cutter, self-healing cutting mat, and acrylic quilting ruler

Large safety pins

Perle cotton in a coordinating color and large-eye embroidery needle (optional)

Basic sewing tools (page 23)

Note: Read "Getting a Color Match" on page 102 if you prefer to print your own fabric for the backing and binding.

design the fabric

1 Prepare the artwork.

For this design, Ellen created an original piece of artwork that is exactly 9 x 10½ inches (23 x 26.5 cm). She chose this size because these dimensions scale up to fit precisely on 1 yard (.9 m) of her chosen fabric, the basic cotton, which is 36 x 42 inches (91 x 107 cm). Note that it's important to choose the kind of fabric you want to print on before creating the design, so you will know the finished size the artwork needs to be—the dimensions of the yard (.9 m) of fabric (length and width) each divided by 4. Create your own artwork based on this formula.

2 Scan and scale the artwork.

Scan the artwork to scale it up from 9 inches (23 cm) to 36 inches (91 cm); revisit the Scaling Formula on page 69 if necessary:

36 INCHES ÷ 9 INCHES = 4; 4 X 150 DPI = 600 DPI

So set the scanner to scan the design at 600 dpi, which gives you enough pixels to scale up from 9 inches to 36 inches. Save the image.

3 Rotate, upload, and print.

Open the file in your graphics software. Because fabric is printed crosswise (page 30), rotate the image so that its long side matches the long side (or width) of the yard (.9 m) of fabric. Select the image and choose "Rotate" or "Image Rotation" from the "Edit" or "Image" menu to rotate it 90°.

Save the file and upload it to Spoonflower (page 18). Choose a centered repeat (page 60).

making the quilt

4 Prepare the fabric.

Wash and dry the fabric. Press to remove any wrinkles. Using the rotary cutter and ruler, cut the binding fabric into 3-inch (7.5 cm) wide strips across the width of the fabric. Trim away the selvedges and set aside.

5 Assemble the quilt layers.

On a large table, lay out the quilt backing fabric with the wrong side up. Use masking tape to secure the backing to the table at the corners and sides of the fabric, stretching it just slightly to remove any wrinkles and make sure it is smooth. Lay the batting on top of the backing and smooth to remove any wrinkles. Center the quilt top (right side up) on top of the other layers. The batting and backing will be larger and should extend past all the edges. Starting from the center, smooth the fabric in place.

6 Baste and trim.

Pin through all the layers to baste them together, placing a safety pin about every 6 inches (15 cm) over the entire quilt. Remove the tape. With a long basting stitch on the sewing machine, stitch ¼ inch (6 mm) from the edge of the quilt top, through all the layers. Trim all the layers to match the edges of the quilt top.

7 Quilt or tie.

Add machine quilting or hand-tie the quilt to keep the layers together. Quilt around large shapes by stitching along the edges with a straight stitch or stitch in an allover pattern like a grid or random swirls. Optionally, you can use perle cotton to make ties over the surface of your quilt, as seen in the photo on the opposite page: Make a small stitch through all the layers and then tie the thread ends in a square knot and trim. Remove the safety pins.

8 Add the binding.

Join four strips of binding together at the short ends, using a ¼-inch (6 mm) seam allowance. Press the seams open and press under ½ inch (1.2 cm) on one short end. Fold the binding strip in half lengthwise and press. Working on the front of the quilt and beginning with the folded short end of the binding, align the raw edges of the binding and the quilt, starting in the center of one long side. Pin the first side and begin to stitch about 2 inches (5 cm) from the folded end, using a ½-inch (1.2 cm) seam allowance. Stitch to within ½ inch (1.2 cm) of the corner; stop your line of stitching and backstitch. Fold the binding strip up and press with your fingers to create a diagonal fold, then fold it back down to align the raw edges along the next side. Stitch and continue in this manner to bind all sides (see Figure 1). When you approach the folded end, lap the raw end of the binding inside the folded end, trimming as needed, and complete the line of stitching.

Fold the binding out, then press and fold it to the back of the quilt, covering the raw edges. Handstitch the binding edge to the back of the quilt.

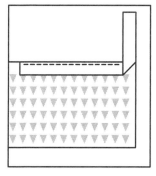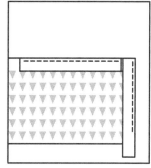

FIGURE 1 Fold the binding strip up so it lines up with the next side you will be stitching to create the diagonal fold. Then with that diagonal fold still in place, fold the length of the binding strip back down and continue stitching, starting at the corner.

MORE IDEAS

✦ Use family photos or kid's art
as the start of your design.
Create your photo collage or
art at the same size Ellen did
in this project and you can
follow the same instructions to
scan and enlarge it for a baby-
sized quilt.

✦ Make coordinating pillows.
Scan the art at full size, 9 x
10½ inches (23 x 26.5 cm),
and print on a fat quarter to
make a cute little pillow that
matches your small quilt.
Trim it down to size, leaving a
seam allowance, and follow
Steps 5–8 of the Portrait
Pillows (page 101) to complete.
Use polyfill or another loose
stuffing to stuff the pillow
since there is no standard
pillow form in this size.

✦ Create a coordinating repeat
for the back of the quilt.
Instead of backing with a
solid-colored fabric, scan
your image (page 68) and
decrease the size of your
design. A really easy way to
do this is to use the Design
Size tool on Spoonflower.
After you have uploaded your
design (page 18) and see the
preview, click the "Smaller"
button to resize the artwork,
reducing it as much as you
like, then choose your favorite
repeat layout (page 60). Both
the "Smaller" button and the
Repeat layouts appear on
the preview screen, so you
can experiment to find the
combination you like best.

Coloring Wallpaper & Desk Wrap

TASHA GODDARD / GLOUCESTERSHIRE, UNITED KINGDOM;
SUZANNE DYE / OREM, UT; AND OLIVIA HENRY / QUEENSLAND, AUSTRALIA

This project idea came from one of Spoonflower's weekly contests. The challenge: design floral coloring book wallpaper. We chose two of the top ten submissions to feature at right: an allover floral by Tasha Goddard (near right) and a mouse floral by Suzanne Dye (far right). They're known as tasha_goddard_design and suzanne_dye, respectively, on our site.

We love the idea of letting the kids (and the kids at heart) color on the walls, but for our photo shoot we decided to improvise a bit and adhered our paper to precut 2 x 6-foot (.6 x 1.8 m) wooden shelving boards from the hardware store (see right). And then we thought, let's color on the furniture too, so we adhered another floral paper designed by Olivia Henry (house_of_henry on the site) to a long desk/arts-and-crafts table we made out of a door (page 127).

When it comes time to print your paper, you can choose either our peel-and-stick wallpaper, which peels off easily when you are ready to take it down, or our water-activated paper, which is more permanent. You can color on either using colored markers, crayons, colored pencils, or pens.

MATERIALS & TOOLS

TO DESIGN THE WALLPAPER
OR DESK WRAP

White paper

Black markers or pens

Peel-and-stick or water-
   activated wallpaper, in
   your preferred amount
   (see Step 3)

TO INSTALL PEEL-AND-STICK
WALLPAPER

Printed wallpaper

Scissors

Pencil

Ruler and level

Burnishing tool (credit card
   or rubber squeegee)

Colored markers, crayons,
   or pens

TO INSTALL WATER-
ACTIVATED WALLPAPER

Printed wallpaper

Scissors

Sponge

Wallpaper tub or trough

Drop cloth (optional)

Colored markers, crayons,
   or pens

designing the wallpaper

1 Create the design.

Draw your design on paper using a black marker or pen. Make a single repeating element or create a seamless repeat (page 62) to fill the whole space. We show three different designs in the various photos for this project. Because wallpaper is typically meant to cover a large area, you might consider a larger repeat, say about 12 x 12 inches (30.5 x 30.5 cm), as long as your scanner bed is large enough. You are going to add color later by treating this design like a coloring book, so your artwork just needs to be black-and-white line drawings.

2 Scan your design.

You choose the settings for this design. Remember that you can scan your design at a higher resolution and enlarge it for your final pattern by scaling (page 69). Or, you can scan and shrink it down by resizing (page 90), depending on the kind of finished design you want to create. Note the difference in scale of the two designs in the photograph on the opposite page, for instance. See the Pixel Equation on page 42 if you need a reminder about the how the variables of pixels, resolution, and size work together.

3 Clean up and upload.

Review the basic information on refining your artwork (pages 114–115). Clean up any flaws in the drawing with the Paintbrush tool (page 114).

Save the file and upload it to Spoonflower (page 18). Choose a swatch of wallpaper if you want to decorate just a small area of your wall—or print a whole roll! One standard roll that is 2 x 12 feet (.6 to 3.7 m) will cover 24 square feet (2.2 square meters).

installing the wallpaper

4 Prepare the surface and apply the wallpaper.

Clean the surface where you are planning to stick your wallpaper and let it dry thoroughly.

PEEL-AND-STICK. Use scissors to trim the wallpaper to your desired size, including an extra 3 to 4 inches (7.5 to 10 cm) in each direction. Draw a straight line on the back of the shelving board or door about 3 inches (7.5 cm) from the top; peel back 1 to 2 inches (2.5 to 5 cm) of the backing paper from the top of the wallpaper strip and place it on the line. Press it to hold in place. Peel away the backing paper as you wrap the wallpaper over the top of the shelving board or door and around to the front. Smooth in place, working from the center out. You can use the edge of a credit card or a rubber squeegee to burnish the paper to the surface and help gently push out any bubbles or wrinkles. Fold the extra wallpaper to the back of the board or door; this allows you to have extra coloring space on the edges of your board or door, too.

WATER-ACTIVATED ADHESIVE. Since this product must be submerged in water and needs to sit for several minutes before it is applied to the wall, you may want to protect the floor in your working area with a drop cloth. Trim the wallpaper to your chosen size with scissors; if you want to wrap the paper around the edges of your board or door as we did, cut extra as described in the peel-and-stick entry. Submerge the wallpaper in the tub or trough of water until it is wet and then remove the strip; now "book" the wallpaper by folding each end toward the middle of the strip with the pasted sides touching. Leave the paper for 3 to 5 minutes while the paste activates, then unfold one end only and smooth it onto your surface. Unfold the remaining end and smooth in place with the sponge.

Wallpaper FYI

Although we didn't hang wallpaper on an entire wall for this project, you may want to. Here's an important note if you do:

Wallpaper designs are a little bit tricky. Because you want each strip to align perfectly with the ones next to it when you hang it, Spoonflower does a little work behind the scenes to resize your design so it repeats exactly across the 24-inch (61 cm) width of the paper, making that matching step easier. Be sure to check the preview when you upload your design so you will know that it is printing the size you want it to be.

If hanging multiple strips, it's a good idea to find a friend to help you; work from left to right and be sure to overlap the strips as Spoonflower recommends. See complete instructions for both types of wallpaper in the "Wallpaper and Gift Wrap" section of our online Help Center: help.spoonflower.com.

MORE IDEAS

+ For cool party favors for kids, print swatches for each child and include a few colorful markers in a goodie bag.

+ Try covering a desk or table instead of a wall. We made a simple coloring table by covering an old door with wallpaper and resting it on two saw horses (see photo at right).

+ Print your black-and-white design on fabric to make a silk kerchief, referring to the information on sizing (page 90) and scaling (page 69) as needed. We printed 1 yard (.9 m) of silk crepe de chine, trimmed it to a 22 x 22-inch (56 x 56 cm) square, and added a simple rolled hem (page 178). Any lightweight fabric would work well for this simple scarf.

+ Make a one-of-a-kind t-shirt. Print your design on one of Spoonflower's knit fabrics, stitch up a simple t-shirt using your favorite sewing pattern, then color in the design with fabric markers.

+ Print on wrapping paper for gift wrap you can personalize with color.

Hand-Drawn Quilt Labels

CYNTHIA FRENETTE / BRITISH COLUMBIA, CANADA

Graphic designer and illustrator Cynthia Frenette (known as cynthiafrenette on Spoonflower) hand-drew the lettering for this delightful label, then completed the design in a graphics program. She left a blank space with dotted lines to add a personal message after it's printed, which makes it possible to use the same label design for more than one quilt. For another label idea, see page 145.

designing the fabric

MATERIALS & TOOLS

TO DESIGN THE FABRIC

Regular pencil

White colored pencil or crayon

Black construction paper

Scanner

Basic graphics program

1 swatch of basic cotton, poplin, or sateen, 8 x 8 inches (20 x 20 cm) (we used poplin)

TO ADD THE LABEL

Basic sewing tools (page 23)

1   Draw the label and add the lettering.

Sketch your label shape on black paper and cut it out; it should be about 4 x 7 inches (10 x 17.5 cm). (Don't worry about the gray part of the design for now—that is added in Step 3.) Draw the letters "I Made This for You" or the message of your choice on the upper half of your label using the white colored pencil or crayon, referring to the photo opposite as a guide. Refine the lettering and add details and flourishes (see page 130 for suggestions about drawing letters). To recreate Cynthia's chalkboard, trace over the letters in your message to make them more bold or fill them in with color; both techniques were used in this drawing.

2   Scan the drawing.

Place your design face down on the scanner and cover it with a sheet of white paper. Scan it at a 1:1 ratio or 150 dpi.

3   Create a new canvas.

Review the basic information on refining your artwork (pages 114–115). Create a new canvas that is 8 x 8 inches (20 x 20 cm) / 1200 x 1200 pixels. "Place" or "Insert" your scanned image and use the Magic Wand to select the background. Choose a color to match your quilt (Cynthia chose blue) and use the Paint Bucket to fill the background area with color. Remember you can use the Color Map (page 50) to help you choose a color by matching a chip to your quilt.

Drawing Letters

If you don't have much experience with hand-drawn letters, here are some pointers to get you started.

To get ideas for shapes of letters or frills you might add to text, look for lettering in magazines and on book covers, in advertisements, on packaging, and on billboards.

Try Googling terms like "hand-lettering," "chalkboard art," and "calligraphy." There are lots of ways to give your letters personality. Experiment with thick and thin lines, the slant of the letter, or the space between letters; add curls or embellishments. Play!

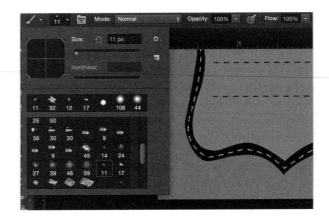

FIGURE 1 Use the Paintbrush tool and the brush of your choice to create the lines for the message.

4 Add the message area.

Use the Lasso tool to create the message area to add the personal information (shown in gray in this project). To do so, carefully trace a shape that mirrors the outside edge of the design; you could also use the Marquee Select tool to select a simple rectangle. Once it is selected, choose a color and fill it with the Paint Bucket.

Add lines to write your message with the Paintbrush tool. Choose a small brush with a rough edge from the Brushes palette to match the "chalkboard" style of Cynthia's design (Figure 1).

5 Save, upload, and print.

Save the image as a .jpg and upload to Spoonflower (page 18). Choose a centered repeat (page 60) and a swatch of poplin; although you can also use basic cotton or sateen, poplin is easiest to write on. Remember that you can adjust the size of your design once uploaded (page 90), should you wish to do so.

stitching on the label

6 Add the label.

Cut out the label, leaving ¼ inch (6 mm) on all sides. Turn under ¼ inch (6 mm) on all sides and press. Stitch the label by hand to a corner or edge of the back of your quilt.

MORE IDEAS

+ If you don't want do your own lettering but want to achieve a hand-drawn look, choose a fancy font that looks hand-drawn. Cynthia likes fontsquirrel.com for finding cool, free fonts to download; every font on fontsquirrel is free for all uses. Rather than writing in the message area of the label, you can also use the Text tool to type your inscription in a new layer.

+ If you don't have black paper, try this trick. Draw your design with a soft black pencil or crayon on regular white paper. Scan it as instructed in Step 2 (Figure 2). When you open it in your graphics program, look first for a command called "Invert," which is sometimes in the Adjustments menu. This will reverse the image, switching the black and white areas of the design, making it look more like a chalkboard (Figure 3).

FIGURE 2 To create the chalkboard look without black paper, first draw your design on white paper with a black pencil or crayon and scan.

FIGURE 3 Next, open your artwork in your graphics program and find the "Invert" command to switch the black and white areas of the design.

Family Portraits Necktie

SAMANTHA COTTERILL / NISKAYUNA, NY

Although she calls upstate New York home now, Samantha Cotterill (known as mummysam on Spoonflower) is originally from England. She acknowledges the European influence in her work, particularly her affinity for drawing what she calls "grumpy old men." But mid-century illustrations, especially those done in portrait style, have a warm place in her heart. She loves this pattern because each character appears to have come straight from a classic children's book. Samantha drew these faces by hand using a fine-point pen and then scanned her artwork to create these intriguing repeats.

designing the fabric

MATERIALS & TOOLS

TO DESIGN THE FABRIC

Pencil or pen

White paper

Scanner

1 yard (.9 m) of poplin, sateen, or silky faille (we used poplin for its crisp body)

TO MAKE THE NECKTIE

Printed fabric

Necktie pattern (page 205)

1 yard (.9 m) woven wool flannel for interlining

Basic sewing kit (page 23)

1 **Create the design.**

This design is made of a number of smaller elements—lots of different faces. There are several factors to consider before you create your drawing:

+ Remember that a necktie is only about 4 inches (10 cm) wide, so make sure the scale of your design suits your goal for the project: If your design is drawn at a small scale, you will see many motifs; if it is at a larger scale, you may only see parts of each design element.

+ Keep the size of your scanner in mind when choosing a repeat size, so your drawing will fit on the scanner bed.

+ This fabric is cut on the bias or diagonal to make the tie, so keep that in mind when creating the art. Read more about bias on page 31.

Make a grid on the paper with faint pencil lines to mark your repeat design space; for example, if you want to draw 8 different faces in two rows, make a grid with four spaces for drawing in each of the two rows. Draw in some light guidelines to help line up elements within the design, marking height or width of each separate drawing, for instance. Draw the individual elements that make up your complete design, using pencil or pen. Although you can add some color to your drawing now, see Step 3 if you prefer to add color after you've saved your image and opened it in your graphics program.

2 Scan your design.

Remember that you can scan your design at a higher resolution and enlarge it for your final pattern (page 69). Or, you can scan and shrink it down by resizing (page 90), depending on the kind of finished design you want to create. You choose the settings for this design.

3 Clean up, add color, and upload.

Review the basic information on refining your artwork (pages 114–115). Clean up any flaws in the drawing with the Paintbrush tool. Then use the Magic Wand or Lasso tools (page 91) to select the elements or areas you want to color and fill each one using the Paint Bucket; paint with the Paintbrush instead for a more hand-drawn look.

Save the file and upload it to Spoonflower (page 18). Choose any repeat layout you like (page 60).

making the necktie

4 Trace and assemble the pattern.

Copy and enlarge the pattern pieces on page 205 and tape them together as needed, using the diamond-shaped markings to align the pieces. You will have a total of five pattern pieces when they are taped together: tie front (made from pieces A, B, C), tie back (made from pieces D, E, F), tie interlining (indicated with a dotted line on A–F), front lining, and back lining.

5 Cut the pieces.

All of the pieces for the tie are cut on the bias (or diagonal grain of the fabric). Look for the grainline arrows on the pattern pieces and align them with the lengthwise grain of the fabric as seen in Figure 1.

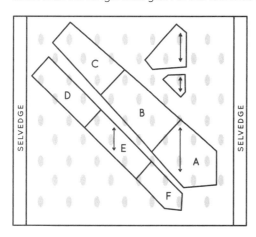

FIGURE 1 **Family Portraits Necktie cutting guide.**

Cut one each of the tie front and back, tie front lining, and tie back lining from your printed fabric.

Cut one tie interlining (indicated by the dotted line on the pattern pieces) from wool flannel.

6 Join tie front and back.

Match the tie front and back centers with right sides together. Stitch using a ¼-inch (6 mm) seam allowance. Press the seam allowance open.

7 Add the lining.

Match the lining front to the tie with right sides together. Stitch the bottom edges only, using a ½-inch (1.2 cm) seam allowance. Trim the corner and turn right side out. Gently push out the tip with a knitting needle or chopstick and press well. Repeat for the tie back lining.

To insert the interlining, lay the tie flat on a table. Insert the tie interlining into the tips of the tie between the tie fabric and lining and pin in place at each tip. Center the interlining on the tie fabric. Fold each raw edge of the tie fabric toward the center, following the edge of the interlining piece as a guide. The raw edges will overlap at the center. Pin generously.

8 Hand-stitch to finish.

To finish the tie, turn under ¼ inch (6 mm) on the raw edge on the top to form the center back seam. Use a slipstitch to sew the seam by hand. Stitch through the back layers of fabric only so the stitches are not visible on the front of the tie.

Hint: Do not press a crease into the folds at the edges of the tie. Let the fabric "roll" around the edge of the interlining without a sharp crease; the tie will hang better and have a more professional-looking finish.

MORE IDEAS

+ If you already have a tie sewing pattern that you like, go ahead and make a tie using that one rather than the one we are providing here. Just design and print your fabric, then follow your pattern instructions.

+ Make a bowtie with this fabric. There are many commercial patterns available at sewing stores; look online, too.

+ Give out these ties to family members for a reunion, wedding, or other special event. For the women in the group, make an Infinity Scarf (page 92) in a matching print.

+ Hand-drawn art like this would make cute notebook or journal covers. See the swatch projects on page 37 for more ideas.

Squid Damask Shower Curtain

BECKA RAHN / MINNEAPOLIS, MN

Damask is an age-old reversible pattern; traditionally, it involves an ornate floral motif woven into the fabric with a monochromatic color scheme. For a modern take on damask, Becka (known as beckarahn on our site) drew a diamond-shaped squid motif on paper with a fine-tipped Sharpie, scanned her artwork, and made a seamless repeat in her graphics program using a very simple blue and white colorway. In Chapter 5, we showed you how to make a seamless repeating tile on paper. In Becka's project, we show you one way to do it digitally.

designing the fabric

MATERIALS & TOOLS

TO DESIGN THE FABRIC

Pencil and fine-tipped Sharpie
White paper
Scanner
5 yards (4.6 m) of linen-cotton canvas, silky faille, eco-canvas, or sateen (we used linen-cotton canvas)

TO MAKE THE SHOWER CURTAIN

Printed fabric
2¼ yards (2.25 m) of 2-inch (5 cm) wide grosgrain ribbon in a coordinating color
Grommets and grommet setting tool
Basic sewing tools (page 23)

1 Create your artwork.

On white paper, use the pencil to lightly sketch a diamond motif to serve as a framework for your damask design. Your diamond motif should be the same size as your drawing; the artwork used in this project was about 8 inches (20 cm) high. Draw your damask pattern with pencil, using the diamond-shaped sketch to help you place the elements. Trace over the lines with the Sharpie. To get the "damask look," think about using bold curving shapes and smooth thick lines.

2 Scan and touch up your artwork.

Review the basic information on refining artwork (pages 114–115). This design was scanned at a 1:1 ratio (meaning full size, 8 inches [20 cm]) at 150 dpi. (Refer to the Scaling Formula on page 69, if necessary.) Open the image in your graphics program and use the Paintbrush tool to clean smudges or stray pencil marks.

3 Create a seamless pattern.

For this design, Becka wanted the squid motifs to be very close to one another, with little space separating them, so she made a seamless tile digitally. To do this, make a new canvas in your graphics program that is about four times larger than your motif so you have plenty of space to work. Using the Lasso tool (page 91), select your image, tracing very close to the edges of the design. Copy that selection and then paste it into your new canvas, using the Move tool (page 91) to put it in the top left corner of the canvas. Paste another copy of the design and move it to the right, aligning the top and bottom edges with your first copy.

Continue to copy and paste until you have 6 copies of your design in 3 staggered lines as in Figure 1 on the next page; one in each corner and one in the center. Carefully align them so they are close together, fitting in like puzzle pieces with tops and edges aligned. Your graphics program may have an option to turn on rulers or a grid to help you line things up (page 183).

Next, crop the tile. Look for a distinctive element in your design (a guide element) to help you place the crop. For this design, we used the left eyeball of the squid as the guide element.

FIGURE 1 To create a seamless pattern, first place 6 copies of your design in three staggered lines, creating a tiny section of what you want the repeat to look like.

Place the four corners of the crop box at exactly the same place on each of the outer four designs in relation to the guide element. Here that means each corner of the crop box is at the center of the squid's left eyeball (Figure 2). After cropping, you have a tile that should repeat seamlessly. You can test the repeat several ways:

+ Open a new canvas and copy and paste this tile, placing the tiles in a grid.

+ Upload and preview it at Spoonflower (page 18).

+ Use the Photoshop Pattern tool (see below).

Check the edges of your design carefully to confirm that the lines are smooth. It is easy to be off by a pixel or two, so you might need to undo and re-crop to get it exactly lined up. This can take a little trial and error.

4 Add color and upload.

Use the Magic Wand tool to select the areas of your design, beginning with the Sharpie outline. Fill it with your preferred color to cover the outline, then fill in the rest of your design with the same color. Select the background color and fill using the Paint Bucket tool for a simple two-color design. Upload your design to Spoonflower (page 18) and choose a basic layout.

FIGURE 2 Next place the 4 corners of the crop box at exactly the same spot on each of the outer 4 designs.

Making a Repeat Pattern in Photoshop

Photoshop and Illustrator both have repeat pattern tools to help you preview or design a repeating pattern. In Photoshop, for example, you can create a basic repeat by selecting an area of the design and choosing "Define Pattern" from the "Edit" menu. This creates the repeat tile. Now open a new file and choose "Fill" from the

"Edit" menu. Find "Pattern" in the drop-down labeled "Contents" and select your custom pattern (Figure 3). The new file will be filled with a basic repeat of the design. Building a repeat pattern in a graphics program allows you to see your pattern before uploading, but it is more involved than using Spoonflower's easy repeat layout tool (page 60).

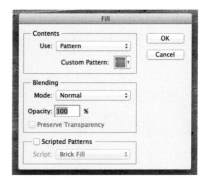

FIGURE 3 The Pattern Fill tool in Photoshop allows you to define a repeat tile and then use it to fill any space.

making the shower curtain

5   Cut the curtain panels.

Cut two pieces that are 78 inches (198 cm) long and the full width of the fabric. Trim away the selvedges. Trim to your desired width: determine the finished width, add 2 inches (5 cm) for seam allowances, divide that number in half, and then cut pieces to that measurement.

6   Connect the two lengths of fabric.

Use a flat-felled seam to create a neat finished seam on the inside of the curtain. Place the long sides of the two pieces of fabric together with right sides facing, stitch with a ½ inch (1.2 cm) seam allowance, and press to one side. Trim the lower seam allowance to ¼ inch (6 mm), turn under ¼ inch (6 mm) on the remaining seam allowance, and fold it over the trimmed seam allowance. Stitch close to the fold (see Figure 4).

7   Add the top ribbon facing.

Along the top edge of the curtain, measure and press a ½-inch (1.2 cm) seam allowance toward the inside of the curtain. Adding the grosgrain ribbon to the top edge creates stability and reinforcement. Match the edge of the ribbon to the folded edge of the fabric and pin in place. Stitch close to both long edges of the ribbon.

8   Hem the edges and bottom.

Turn under a ¼-inch (6 mm) seam allowance on each side edge of the curtain and press. Turn in another ¼ inch (6 mm), folding the raw edge to the inside. Press and stitch close to the inner folded edge.

Press under ½ inch (1.2 cm) at the bottom of the curtain. Fold under an additional 5 inches (12 cm), press, and stitch close to the inner fold.

9   Add grommets.

Follow the instructions on the package to install the grommets along the top edge of the curtain. Space the grommets about 6 to 8 inches (15 to 20 cm) apart (12 to 14 total grommets) and center them in the ribbon facing. If using a plastic liner inside the curtain, you may want to use it to mark your grommet placement or to determine how many you need.

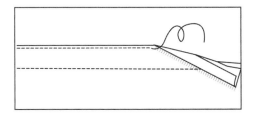

FIGURE 4 Stitching a flat-felled seam assures that the inside of the curtain (the side you'll see when you are showering) looks as finished as the outside.

MORE IDEAS

+ Lots of different types of artwork will work for this project. For example, we bet that Daphne and her friends would love to see their artwork from the napkins on page 116 on a shower curtain.

+ If you're not sure how small or large to make your artwork so that it will look good in your bathroom, make your best guess and then print a swatch to preview before investing in yardage. You can also check color this way.

+ One way to test a lot of colorways of the same design is to fill 1 yard (.9 m) of fabric with a few repeats in each of your color options, which is taught in detail in the pillowcase project on page 189. Just as a reminder, Spoonflower has a great tool to help you do this in another way, too: When you upload each proposed colorway of your design, choose "Create a Collection." You can then print a sampler that shows you a swatch of each design, all on one piece of fabric (page 52). It's an economical way to play with color, as each collection can contain up to 30 designs.

READ ALL ABOUT IT
Design with Words, Text & Layers

SKILLS LEARNED
IN THIS CHAPTER
+ Using the Text tool

+ Using the Spoonflower
  Color Map

+ Using Layers

OPPOSITE Memorable
quotes about dining well
inspired our table runner
(page 149).

Words and numbers have intrinsic artistic and communicative value and can inspire very cool designs. They can be hand-drawn or computer-generated. They can be used to tell a story and personalize a design (see Kim's Simple Quilt Label on page 145) or they can be used to create abstract patterns (as on the Typographic Wrapping Paper on page 153).

In this chapter, we introduce the idea of working in layers, which means creating the different parts of a design (such as background, type, or motifs) as separate elements so that you can manipulate each piece independently of the others.

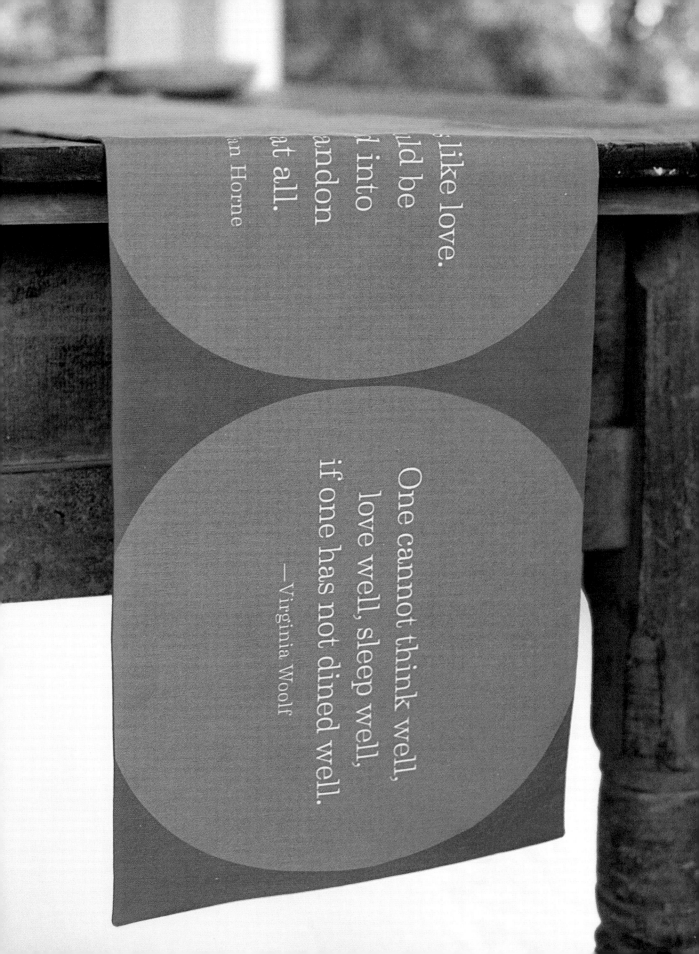

like love.
ld be
l into
andon
at all.
an Horne

One cannot think well,
love well, sleep well,
if one has not dined well.

—Virginia Woolf

Text Tool

The Text tool has a lot of different looks, but the icon is usually something alphabetical, such as a T. As you might guess, the Text tool is used to add text to your designs.

To add text, select the Text tool, click and hold down your mouse, and drag it across the canvas to create a text box in the document. Then type the text into the box. There are generally lots of options for changing text, so it usually has its own panel or palette (a set of additional functions) with the choices for font, size, color, etc. (Figure 1). The best way to change the text is to select the part of the text to style—click and drag to highlight it—and then choose the options you want to change. For instance, you can make your type bold or italic, change the color, or switch to an entirely different font.

Once you have added text, you can use many tools to manipulate it. You can select the text box and move it around, and you can also rotate it; look for arrows or a handle in the selection box to change its direction. In your graphics program, look for additional ways to transform text, as they can vary quite a bit from program to program. There are likely a variety of options built into your software, such as making the text flow in wavy lines or follow a shape that you specify.

Adjusting Color

You can choose text colors in a variety of ways. Use the Text tool palette, as just described; use the Eyedropper tool (as explained on page 114); and don't forget the Spoonflower Color Map (page 50). To use the Color Map, select a color from the map, click on the color palette for the Text tool, then type the code on the Color Map into the box labeled # or HEX (Figure 2).

Using Layers

A design can be built out of many separate layers (for example, one layer can be a background color, another layer can be motifs, and another layer can be text). When the layers are combined, the whole design comes together. At first, working in layers might seem complicated, but before long, you'll see that it is easy and can actually simplify the design process a lot.

What can you do with layers?

+ Change the order of layers to easily rearrange elements that overlap one another. If you're composing a design with leaves on one layer and daisies on the other, you can quickly experiment with the composition to decide if you want the leaves in front of—or behind—the daisies.

+ Duplicate layers to make copies of an element. For example, draw a single daisy and then make many copies of it to scatter all over the design. Instead of copying and

FIGURE 1 Type in your text and customize as you like with the Text tool.

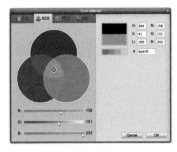

FIGURE 2 If you have the Spoonflower Color Map (page 50), you can type in the code for your desired color in the palette for your Text tool.

pasting many daisies, which can leave a hole in your background and can put them in a permanent position in your design, you can have the individual images on layers to move or manipulate independently without affecting the other layers in your design. It's also easy to delete a daisy or two if you decide you don't want them!

+ Change the placement of an entire layer without having to select each individual element. Back to our daisies and leaves example for a moment; suppose you wanted all the daisies to shift to the left? It's a breeze to move the entire layer at once rather than working on each element separately.

+ Make layers visible or invisible to test out variations on your design. Let's imagine that you are working on your daisies and leaves composition but wonder about the distribution of the daisies. To work on that element only, you can make the leaves layer invisible so you can concentrate on the flowers.

+ Add or delete layers or apply effects like color overlays, drop shadows, or transparency to individual layers. Layers give you the freedom to tweak your original design by adding all sorts of intriguing effects; you may recall that we added a texture to a variation of the design used in the Color Chip Lampshade project (page 77).

+ Create different colorways of one design by putting all of the elements that are the same color together on one layer. In Figures 3 and 4 the text, dots, and background from our Food for Thought Table Runner (page 149) are each on a different layer. You can change the color of each layer by adding a "Color Overlay" and all of the elements in the selected layer change color at the same time, so you don't have to select each element individually. It's a quick way to experiment with color.

The Layers tool usually has a panel or palette that will pop up on your screen, which consists of a variety of functions as do the palettes associated with other tools. (In Photoshop, if the tool doesn't pop up automatically, look under the "Window" menu item for "Layers.") To add a new layer, find the symbol in the palette that looks like a blank piece of paper, or choose "New Layer" in the menu (Figure 5).

To change the order of layers, just click and drag them around in the palette in the order you like. The small eyeball symbol that is next to the layer makes it visible; click to make it become invisible.

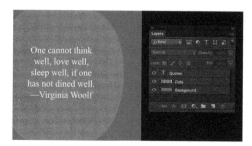

FIGURE 3 Placing the text, dots, and background in different layers allows you to manipulate each one separately.

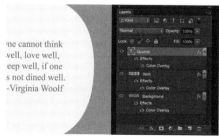

FIGURE 4 Note the words "Color Overlay" and the eyeball icon under each layer, telling you that an overlay was applied to the original colors.

FIGURE 5 To add a new layer, find the symbol that looks like a blank piece of paper.

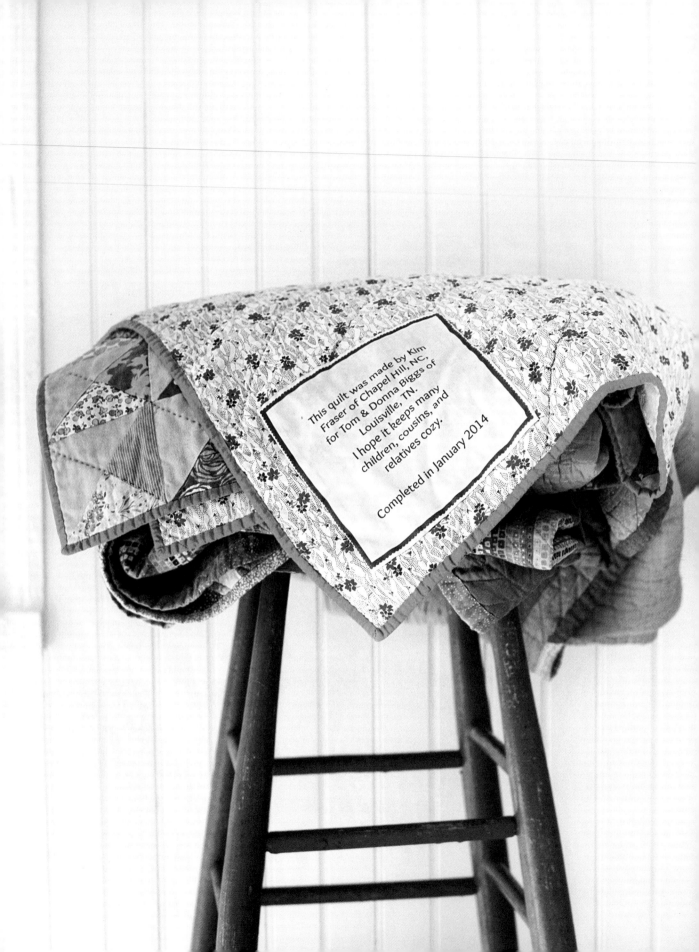

This quilt was made by Kim
Fraser of Chapel Hill, NC,
for Tom & Donna Biggs of
Louisville, TN.
I hope it keeps many
children, cousins, and
relatives cozy.

Completed in January 2014

Kim's Simple Quilt Label

KIM FRASER / CHAPEL HILL, NC

Kim Fraser (known as kimspoonflower on the site) is the wife of Spoonflower co-owner Stephen Fraser. She took a hand-quilting class at a local quilt store when she was pregnant with her second daughter and she has been quilting ever since. Making the label is always an important final step for Kim because she uses it to tell a part of the quilt's story, and to make the quilt even more meaningful for years—maybe generations—to come. Kim created this simple yet eloquent label in PicMonkey. You can use the same technique for making labels of any size, even small ones to stitch into clothing.

designing the fabric

MATERIALS & TOOLS

TO DESIGN THE FABRIC

Basic graphics program

1 swatch of basic cotton, poplin, or sateen, 8 x 8 inches (20 x 20 cm) (we used basic cotton)

TO ADD THE LABEL

Basic sewing tools (page 23)

1 Create a new canvas.

Create a new canvas in your graphics program that is 8 x 8 inches (20 x 20 cm) / 1200 x 1200 pixels.

2 Add a background frame.

Review the instructions for working with text and layers (pages 142–143). If your graphics program has an option to add a frame to a canvas, as Kim's did, choose a frame with scalloped edges or the frame of your choice. Kim matched the border color to the quilt, using the color tools in her graphics program. (If you don't have an option to add a border from within your graphics program, you can find a copyright-free clip-art border online. (To find clip art, do a Google search for "free clip art" or "copyright-free imagery" online.) If you would like an exterior border of white as in Kim's design, reduce the size of your frame to leave ½ inch (1.2 cm) on all sides (Figure 1).

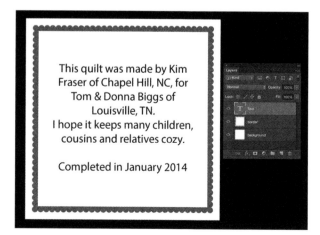

This quilt was made by Kim Fraser of Chapel Hill, NC, for Tom & Donna Biggs of Louisville, TN.
I hope it keeps many children, cousins and relatives cozy.

Completed in January 2014

FIGURE 1 This design uses three layers: one for the background, one for the border, and one for the text.

READ ALL ABOUT IT

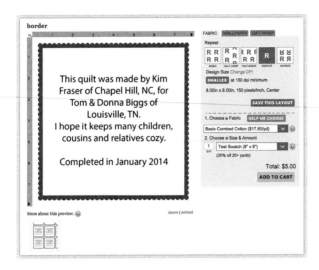

This quilt was made by Kim
Fraser of Chapel Hill, NC, for
Tom & Donna Biggs of
Louisville, TN.
I hope it keeps many children,
cousins and relatives cozy.

Completed in January 2014

FIGURE 2 Upload your
file, then choose swatch
and centered repeat.

3 Add a text layer.

Add your message with the Text tool (page 142). Kim chose a centered
alignment and chose black for the color of her text (Figure 2). Read her
text above and then decide what you want your message to be.

4 Save, upload, and print.

Save the file and upload it to Spoonflower (page 18). Print one label on
a swatch using a centered repeat. Or you can make multiple labels by
choosing a different repeat layout (page 60) and/or printing on 1 yard
(.9 m) of fabric. Choose a smooth, tightly woven fabric like poplin if you
think you might use a fabric pen to add a handwritten message on your
labels.

stitching on the label

5 Add the label.

Turn under ¼ inch (6 mm) on all sides and press. Stitch the label by hand
to a corner or edge of the back of your quilt.

SPOONFLOWER DESIGNERS READ ALL ABOUT IT

It's easy to take letters and numbers for granted as we see and use them constantly in our everyday lives. Thinking about them as design elements creates a unique, exciting challenge. The designers whose work is featured here drew upon them as organic shapes, as branding devices, as vision tests, and as a drawing tool to create black-and-white, positive and negative space. They used computer-generated, handwritten, and typewritten letters and numbers on their own and in combination with other forms, in one-color, two-color, and multicolor designs. What's next? That's for you to decide. We hope you'll upload your creations to the Spoonflower site so we can enjoy them.

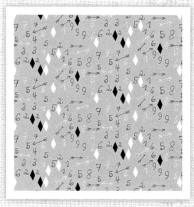

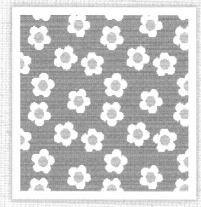
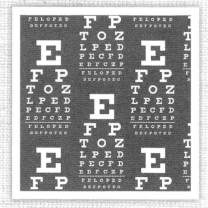

LEFT COLUMN, FROM TOP

ALEX MORGAN
(spellstone)

HOLLI ZOLLINGER
(holli_zollinger)

KELLY HARMAN
(weavingmajor)

RIGHT COLUMN, FROM TOP

ANDA CORRIE
(anda)

SHELLEY AKAJAR
(shelleymade)

HOLLI ZOLLINGER
(holli_zollinger)

Cooking is like love. It should be entered into with abandon or not at all.

—Harriet Van Horne

If you're afraid of butter, use cream.

—Julia Child

Savor the ritual of the table. Mealtime is a time for empathy and generosity, a time to nourish and communicate.

—Alice Waters

Food for Thought Table Runner

We created oversized Os that we thought looked like dinner plates and filled them with some of our favorite food- and cooking-related quotes to create this fun table runner, sure to be a conversation piece at any gathering. Of course, you can create your table runner based the theme of your choice. How about names of family members, lines from favorite poems or songs, or a word of welcome in several languages.

designing the fabric

MATERIALS & TOOLS

TO DESIGN THE FABRIC
Basic graphics program
Ruler or measuring tape
2 yards (2 m) of linen-cotton
canvas, sateen, basic cotton,
or faux suede (we used linen-
cotton canvas) (see Note)

TO MAKE THE TABLE RUNNER
Printed fabric
2 yards (2 m) of lightweight
fabric for backing
Knitting needle, chopstick,
or point turner
Basic sewing tools (page 23)

Note: Because of the size
of a table runner, you will
need to rotate this design
90° to print lengthwise on
2 yards (2 m) of fabric. If
you repeat the design, you
can make 3 runners from
the same 2 yards of fabric,
because you'll have plenty
of width.

1 Create a new canvas.

Before you create your canvas in your graphics program, decide what size to make your table runner. Measure your table if you want to create a custom-sized table runner; a standard-size runner is 70 x 14 inches (177.8 x 35.6 cm). Add 1 inch (2.5 cm) to your length and width measurements to allow for a ½-inch (1.2 cm) seam allowance. For the standard table runner, that means you need a canvas that is 71 x 15 inches (180.5 x 38 cm) / 10,650 x 2250 pixels. (We used the Pixel Equation on page 42 to determine the canvas size.)

2 Create the background.

Review the instructions for working with text and layers (page 142). This design is created in three layers: the background, the circles, and the text. First, fill the background layer with your preferred color, using the Paint Bucket tool (page 115).

Make a new layer for the large dots design. For our project, they were created using the letter O that was filled in with the same color as the font, using the Eyedropper and Paint Bucket tools from Chapter 8 (pages 114–115). You could also use the bullet (•) or asterisk (*) character to create the dots. Place them evenly across your canvas, either leaving a ½ inch (1.2 cm) margin at the edges for a seam allowance or allowing the shapes to extend off the edges of the canvas, as we did.

3 Add the quotes.

Add a third layer and use the Text tool to place your quotes. For a list of the quotes we used, see page 150.

4 Rotate, save, and upload.

Rotate the image in your graphics program so that its long side matches the length of the fabric. To do so, select all of the layers and choose an option from the menu to rotate the canvas 90°. (You may need to combine the layers before you rotate. Look for a command called "Merge" or "Flatten.") If you are working in Photoshop it is a good idea to save this as a .psd file before you merge layers to make it easy to edit again later.

Save the file and upload it to Spoonflower (page 18). Choose a fabric—we used linen-cotton canvas—and a centered or basic repeat (page 60).

making the table runner

5 Prepare your fabric.

Wash, dry, and press your fabric and backing fabric. Trim your table runner to size, being sure to include the seam allowances. Cut a piece of backing fabric that is the same size as your runner.

6 Stitch and clip.

Place your runner and backing fabric with right sides together. Match the raw edges and pin. Stitch using a ½-inch (1.2 cm) seam allowance, pivoting at the corners and leaving a 4-inch (10 cm) opening in one long side for turning. Clip the corners.

7 Turn and press.

Turn the runner right side out, using a knitting needle, chopstick, or point turner to help push out the corners. Press. Slipstitch the opening.

As an optional finish, add topstitching in a coordinating or contrasting color. Stitch around all sides ¼ inch (6 mm) from the edge with a sewing machine or stitch by hand with a running stitch and embroidery thread.

Food for Thought

These are the six quotes we printed on our table runner.

Everything you see I owe to spaghetti.

—Sophia Loren

First we eat, then we do everything else.

—M. F. K. Fisher

Savor the ritual of the table. Mealtime is a time for empathy and generosity, a time to nourish and communicate.

—Alice Waters

If you're afraid of butter, use cream.

—Julia Child

Cooking is like love. It should be entered into with abandon or not at all.

—Harriet Van Horne

One cannot think well, love well, sleep well, if one has not dined well.

—Virginia Woolf

If you're
afraid of butter,
use cream.

—Julia Child

Cooking is
It shou
entered
with aba
or not a

—Harriet Va

Typographic Wrapping Paper

SARAH GIFFORD / MAPLEWOOD, NJ

Sarah Gifford, who is sarahgdesign on our site, Daphne's mom (page 116), and the graphic designer of this book, had a lot of fun creating these wrapping papers using just one humble punctuation mark: the exclamation point. By varying the font, size, color, and style of it, she transformed it into a fascinating design motif. Any letter or number or symbol will work. Think about your initial or your lucky number, ampersands, asterisks, question marks—the sky is the limit, especially if you consider the writing systems of many different cultures.

designing the wrapping paper

MATERIALS & TOOLS

TO DESIGN THE PAPER

Basic graphics program
1 roll of gift wrap, 26 x
   72 inches (66 x 183 cm)
   (see Note)

Note: Spoonflower's gift wrap is available only in rolls. You can wrap about 4 medium-sized gifts per roll. Order more if you need it!

1 Make a new canvas.

Create a new canvas that is 8 x 8 inches (20 x 20 cm) / 1200 x 1200 pixels or the size you prefer. Remember that the Pixel Equation is on page 42 if you need to review it.

2 Create your design.

Review the instructions for working with text and layers (pages 142–143). To create your typography design, use the exclamation mark as shown here or choose a different letter, number, or symbol that you want to feature. Then search around for different fonts, if you don't have a wide selection already; see page 131 for advice on finding free fonts.

As mentioned on page 142, each graphics program has its own way of dealing with text. Although these designs were created in Adobe Illustrator (a vector-based program you'll learn more about in the next chapter), you can use the Text tool and/or Layers in any program to create similar effects with text, including moving and rotating individual characters, changing colors, and so on. You can have a lot of fun designing with just one character in whichever program you have! And remember that Spoonflower has built-in repeat layouts (page 60) and a Color Change tool (page 53), so you could upload a design based on just a few characters and let Spoonflower do the work for you.

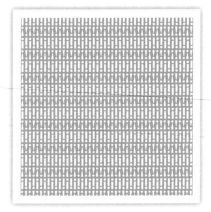 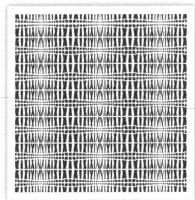 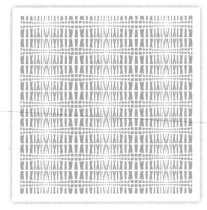

If you want to make Sarah's designs, here is how she created each design shown in the photo on page 152:

PINK PAPER. To create this striped effect, use two different fonts. To begin, make a background rectangle the size of your design and color it pink (or the color of your choice); choose white (or another color of your choice) for the type. Type an exclamation point in the first font; copy and paste it, then rotate the second exclamation point upside down. Align the two exclamation points, select each of their text boxes, and copy them as a unit. Paste this unit next to the first set of exclamation points, and continue in this fashion until you've created a row. Repeat to create a new row in the second font, alternating the placement of the upside-down exclamation point. When both rows are finished, copy the text boxes for each row and paste your rows to fill the canvas.

BLUE & GREEN DESIGNS ON WHITE PAPER. Both of these colorways are created in the same way. Choose a font that has many styles, choose a color from the Text tool palette, and type an exclamation point in every variation of the font one after the other: bold, italic, light, condensed, and so on. Depending on the graphics program you use, you may be able to adjust the space between the exclamation points, too, as was done here. Copy and paste your collection of exclamation points to fill an entire row in your canvas. When uploading to Spoonflower, choose a mirrored repeat.

LAVENDER PAPER & YELLOW PAPER. Both of these colorways are created in the same way. Create a background color and choose white type (or type in the color of your choice) as described in the instructions for the pink paper. Copy and paste an exclamation point until you have eight, then select and rotate each one individually to align the dots at the center, making a flower shape. Add an exclamation point that is the same height as the flower shape, adjusting the height or size of the flower shape as needed. Copy and paste the exclamation point and flower shape to the right of your original, then rotate one of the large exclamation points 180° so it is upside down. Copy and paste these elements to fill an entire row. Then copy and paste the row to fill the canvas.

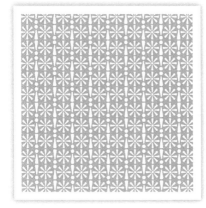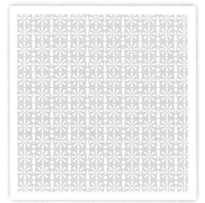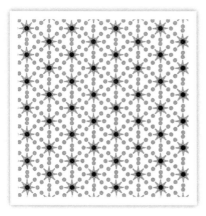

GRAY-ON-GRAY DESIGNS ON WHITE PAPER. This design is the inverse of that used in the lavender and yellow papers, as the top of the exclamation marks are aligned instead of the dots. Build the design as for the lavender and yellow papers, filling your entire design space, making all the layers transparent so they combine to create the darker shade in the center. Look for an "opacity" setting to adjust transparency.

To make a seamless repeat (page 62) for these patterns, carefully arrange your design so you can split an exclamation point in half at the edge of your canvas. If your particular design makes this a little tricky, here's an alternative: Make your design fill the entire canvas but leave one-half the amount of space between your exclamation points (or other design elements) around all sides. For example, if there is ¼ inch (6 mm) between each of your exclamation marks, then leave a ⅛-inch (3 mm) margin of empty space around the design. When printed, the margins you left will equal the spacing between your designs—⅛ inch (3 mm) + ⅛ inch (3 mm) = ¼ inch (6 mm).

Have fun with this project! You can copy, paste, rotate, and layer your individual elements (or rows of elements) to build a design, placing them as you wish.

3 **Save and upload.**

Save the file and upload it to Spoonflower (page 18). If a repeat layout wasn't suggested for your particular design in Step 2, try them all to see which effect you like best.

Monogrammed Stickers

Once Sarah had finished designing the wrapping paper, she still wanted to play with the exclamation point a bit more, so she decided to add these stickers to her collection. She used the exclamation points as a frame and then placed a letter inside each frame. These can be used with or without the wrapping paper. Here we show them on packages, envelopes, and notebooks.

To make a sticker, size your canvas for a swatch of peel-and-stick wallpaper, 24 x 12 inches (61 x 30.5 cm) / 3600 x 1800 pixels. Sarah worked in Illustrator; to re-create her design, do the following: Draw a background square and fill it with your chosen color. Draw a circle within the square (we explain how to create vector shapes like a square and a circle on page 161) and select the Type on a Path tool, which looks like a letter on a sloped or wavy line. Click on the circle, and type a row of exclamation points around the circle and make them white. Draw another circle to fill the center of the design and make it white. With the Text tool, type the letter of your choice inside the circle, matching the color of the square. (Of course, if desired, you can always reverse the colors.)

If you are working in another graphics program you can place and rotate the characters individually to build the frame, as was used to make the flower shape in the lavender and yellow papers (see 154), and you can use the Text tool to add the initial in the center. Use your available tools to draw shapes and add color as desired.

Add as many designs as you want to your canvas, being sure to leave a little extra space around each one to have room to cut them out.

MORE IDEAS

Use the same technique to make many other kinds of personalized stickers:

+ To/from gift tags or shipping labels

+ Labels for jars of homemade jelly or salsa

+ Book plates

+ Inspirational quotes for your desk or bathroom mirror

ABOVE Sarah chose to place multiple monograms on one canvas and had them printed together on a single swatch.

THE WORLD OF VECTORS
All-Digital Designs

OPPOSITE One easy way
to create a vector image
is to trace an element from
a photo. Here we used that
technique to create a new
version of a monogrammed
hankie.

So far, we have been working with raster-based images only—that is, images made up of pixels (page 41), such as photos and scanned artwork. Now we are heading in a slightly differently direction and teaching you how to work with vector-based images—artwork created solely on the computer. When you work with vectors, you have a lot of flexibility to scale designs to any size without compromising quality and you can create precise geometric patterns with smooth outlines because they are based on mathematical formulas. Learning these techniques opens up a new world of possibilities!

What Are Vectors?

Vectors are made by creating shapes defined by a mathematical formula. Imagine a set of pins and rubber bands. You arrange the pins in the shape that you want to create, and then you stretch the bands between the points. The rubber bands can curve around the pins and you can fiddle with them to adjust the shape of the curves. You can "stretch" a vector to any size without it looking jagged, blurry, or pixelated because the vector image is converted to pixels only when printed (see page 41 for more detail).

Graphic designers often like to work in vectors when creating digital art that needs to be constantly scaled up or down. For example, a logo created using vectors can be used on a small clothing tag as well as a giant billboard and still look exactly the same. Compare Figures 1 and 2 to see what happens when each type of image is enlarged.

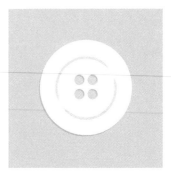

FIGURE 1 If you draw a button in a vector program, you can use it at any size and the quality will be the same.

FIGURE 2 If you draw the same button in a raster program, you can use it at the size you draw it or smaller; if you try to make it larger, it will pixellate, as shown here.

A Very Simple Guide to Drawing with Vectors

To work with vector images you need to have a graphics program designed specifically for this purpose, such as Adobe Illustrator or Inkscape. While Adobe Photoshop has some simple vector-drawing tools built in that might suit your needs, they are limited in scope.

Here is an overview of the tools you'll need to start drawing with vectors. On page 203 is an exercise you can do if you want to practice making a vector image.

PEN TOOL

This is the tool you'll use most often to draw vector images. It looks like an old-fashioned fountain pen.

Click with the Pen tool to create a pin or point. When you click to make the next pin, the two pins will be connected with a stretchy line.

See the practice exercise on page 203 for more details. A good rule of thumb: When making a shape, place a pin at every point where your line has a major change of direction. To finish your design, click back at the original pin to close the shape.

FIGURE 3 Use the Pen tool to draw a vector image and refine it with the Select tool.

SELECT TOOL

The Select tool often looks like a solid black arrow.

When you click an object you've drawn with the Select tool, you select the whole object as a unit and you can move, resize, and rotate it as one piece. For example, if you draw a simple square by connecting four dots, you can move the square around your design space by clicking it with the Select tool and dragging. Resizing is easy: Select the object and click and drag on the toggles (the little boxes) at the corners of the selection to make it larger or smaller.

DIRECT SELECT TOOL

The Direct Select tool looks like an outlined or white arrow.

Direct Select is used to select individual points or pins in your vector design. When you select an individual pin, you can move that specific point to adjust the shapes, curves, and lines. For example, if you create a square and want to turn it into a parallelogram, you can select one bottom pin and drag it, then the opposite bottom pin and drag it, to extend the bottom of the shape.

USING THE ARRANGE FUNCTION

Vector images work similarly to layers (page 142), where different parts of a design exist as separate elements. You organize them with a menu item labeled "Arrange" or "Order." To change the order of the elements in a design, select the object and then use the "Forward" and "Backward" options to move it to the front or back (Figure 4). "Arrange" functions the same way as changing layers but uses a different vocabulary.

SHAPES

Vector programs often have tools or functions that will make basic shapes like squares, circles, polygons, or stars. These tools make drawing a snap! See how we used them in the Pet Silhouette Hankies project on page 176.

Saving Vector Files

Most vector-based programs have their own file formats. For example, Adobe Illustrator's format is .ai. Although Spoonflower printers can work with some of these vector file types, ultimately they need to be converted to a .jpg for the printers to understand what to print. If your program saves your vector files in a proprietary format such as .ai, choose a "Save As" or "Export" option to save it as a .jpg.

You will also probably have an option to choose the resolution to save or export your file so the vectors can be converted to pixels. Remember that digital printers like our inkjet machines need to have pixel-based images to print (page 41.) This works exactly as it does with scanning. If you want the image to print at a 1:1 ratio (full size), you want to export at 150 ppi (page 42).

FIGURE 4 The Arrange function allows you to manipulate different elements of a design separately.

Geometric Soiree Kitchen Chairs

LISA BARRETT / CANBERRA, AUSTRALIA

Although Lisa Barrett studied fashion and textiles years ago, she never imagined that she could design fabric herself . . . until she tried it with Spoonflower! Now, Lisa (known as ninaribena on our site) runs Tango & James, an interior design studio where she rescues old pieces of furniture and uses her fabrics to give them new life. When designing upholstery fabric, Lisa suggests that you create prints that complement the shapes in the piece of furniture you're refurbishing.

MATERIALS & TOOLS

TO DESIGN THE FABRIC

Vector-based graphics program

1 yard (.9 m) of heavy cotton twill, basic cotton, linen-cotton canvas, sateen, or faux suede (we used heavy cotton twill) (see Note)

TO COVER THE CUSHION

Printed fabric

Chair with removable seat

Paint in a matching color (optional)

Washable fabric-marking pen or chalk

Staple gun and staples

Screwdriver

Fabric scissors

Note: The amount of fabric you need will vary depending on the size of your chair(s). Measure the length and width of the chair cushion and add about 5 inches (12 cm) on all sides so that you have enough fabric to wrap around to the bottom of the cushion. Unless your chair is very small, you will almost always need 1 yard (.9 m) of fabric, as a fat quarter will not be enough.

designing the fabric

1 **Create a new canvas.**

Review the information about vector-based images on pages 160–161. This simple geometric design is created by cropping out a part of a collage of vector shapes and then using a mirrored or other repeat on Spoonflower to make a seamless geometric design; your final design can be any size you wish. Create a new canvas that is larger than the finished design size so that you have space to work—at least several inches (cm) on each side so you have some room for cropping.

2 **Add some vector shapes.**

Using the Pen tool, create some basic geometric shapes. Copy and paste to create more shapes and arrange them in a pattern you like. For the fabric shown here, Lisa drew a hexagonal shape about 1 inch (2.5 cm) tall and filled it with a green color she chose from the color palette in her graphics program (page 48). See the collage she created from this basic shape and cropped in Figure 1, below.

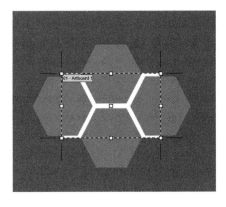

FIGURE 1 The highlighted part of the collage was saved, uploaded to Spoonflower, and repeated to create the honeycomb effect seen on the fabric.

3 Crop your design.

Crop out a part of the collage design (Figure 1). Note that some vector programs do not have a Crop tool per se, but when you export your artwork as a .jpg, the program will automatically crop the design following the edges of the canvas or "artboard" instead. As you create your design, keep in mind that anything outside of this design space will get cropped away, so you can extend your design elements off the artboard to "crop" them.

4 Save and upload design.

Save the design and upload it to Spoonflower (page 18). Try each repeat layout (page 60) to see what sort of cool pattern results and pick your favorite. (If you're really inspired, you can create several coordinating geometric prints by cropping a variety of areas from your collage and using different styles of repeat for each when you upload to Spoonflower, as shown in Figure 2.)

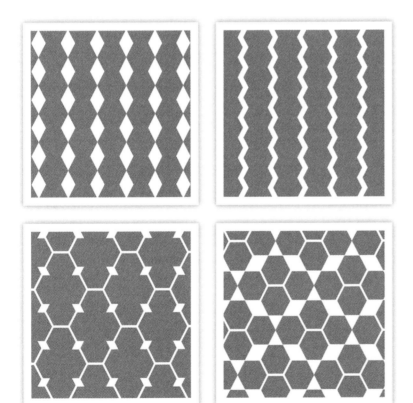

FIGURE 2 An assortment of designs that can be created by adjusting the original collage and changing the repeat pattern.

covering the cushion

5 Prepare the chair.

Remove the chair seat cushion from the chair. These are often held in place with a few screws or bolts between the seat and chair frame. Set aside the screws in a safe place so you don't lose them! If you want to paint the chair itself, as we did for this project, take a swatch of your fabric to the paint store and have them mix a custom color to match. Or remember that you can use the Color Map when creating your design to find a color that matches your paint (page 50). Paint the chair and let dry before reattaching the seat.

6 Cut the fabric.

Remove the fabric cover from the chair cushion and use it as a pattern piece to cut the new fabric. If you are not able to remove the previous cover, place the cushion facedown on your printed fabric and trace around it, including an extra 5 to 6 inches (12 to 15 cm) on each side to wrap around to the bottom of the seat.

7 Attach the fabric.

Starting at one side of the seat, smooth and wrap the fabric to the bottom of the seat and secure with staples. Pull the fabric tautly to remove any wrinkles and then secure the opposite side. Continue in the same manner to staple the remaining sides. Depending on the shape of the chair, you may need to trim away a little of the extra fabric at the corners or ease it around curves. Use the previous cover as a guide if you can.

8 Finish.

Test the fit of your seat on to the chair frame and trim away any excess fabric. Reattach the chair seat to the frame.

Choosing a Print Size for Upholstery and Other Decorating Fabric

Choosing a print (or pattern) size is a personal aesthetic choice, but here are a couple of ideas to keep in mind when designing home-dec fabric.

+ A large-scale print can help a piece of furniture pop and stand out, while smaller-scale prints tend to blend in visually. Many decorators recommend using at least three patterns in any room—one large-scale pattern with many colors for visual impact, a second pattern that is about half the size with fewer colors, and a third smaller pattern that creates balance between the other two with just a few colors: Think of a large floral, a medium plaid, and a smaller geometric.

+ Taking simple geometric prints, such as a square, diamond, or polka dot, to a larger scale can create visual interest and importance. If you recall the story we told you in the introduction about Kim Fraser wanting giant-size dots, this is what started Spoonflower in the first place! Read about Kim's idea on page 7 if you missed it.

Leaves Table Wrap

ALLISON JANSSEN / LAGUNA BEACH, CA

If you visit us at Spoonflower headquarters in North Carolina, you'll likely notice that we like to dress up our furniture with our peel-and-stick paper. For this table wrap, we looked for a design in the Spoonflower marketplace and were happy to find Golden Leaves by Allison Janssen (known as fable_design on our site). A former art director at a greeting card company, Allison now runs a freelance design/illustration business. She describes her style as bright, whimsical, happy, modern, and always a bit imperfect. A few leaves picked up off the ground during a run inspired this design, proving once again that inspiration is everywhere.

We've written the instructions so that you can understand how Allison created her leaf shapes, but of course, you can create whatever shape you desire. Look around you to see what interests you—flowers, faces, birds, bottles, shoes, spiders, etc.—and make your drawing as simple or as complicated as you like. If you're just beginning to draw in a vector program, you might be more comfortable with basic shapes like Allison's leaves, but as your confidence grows, so might the complexity of your ideas.

MATERIALS & TOOLS

TO DESIGN THE WALLPAPER / TABLE WRAP

Vector-based graphics program

1 roll of peel-and-stick wallpaper, 2 x 12 feet (.6 x 3.7 m) (see Note)

TO INSTALL THE TABLE WRAP

Printed wallpaper

Flexible tape measure

Scissors

Pencil

Ruler and level

Burnishing tool (credit card or rubber squeegee)

Note: Depending on the size of the piece of furniture you're wrapping, you may need only a swatch (24 x 12 inches [61 x 30.5 cm]) rather than an entire roll. Measure the length and width of the area you wish to decorate as in Step 6 to decide how much you need to order.

designing the wallpaper/wrap

1 **Create a new canvas.**

Review the information about vector-based images on pages 160–161. To give yourself room for repeating elements, create a new file that is about 4 times the size of the main element. In this design, the leaves are about 5 inches (12 cm) tall, so we made our file 20 x 20 inches (50 x 50 cm) / 3000 x 3000 pixels.

2 **Draw the solid leaf shape (or shape of your choice).**

This design has two versions of the leaf motif. The solid one is filled in with color (yellow) while other is just an outline. Draw the solid shape first; use the Pen tool to create a single leaf shape. Since vector shapes can have a fill and an outline color (page 115), select the leaf shape and fill it with a color, but choose "no color" for the outline. (The "no color" selection usually looks like a box with a red line through it, as shown on page 203.)

3 **Draw the leaf outline (or outline of your choice).**
To make the leaf outline, select, copy, and paste the solid leaf shape. Select and move the original solid leaf shape aside into the margin of the canvas for now. Working on the pasted shape, select it and choose to fill with no color and outline with black. Use the Pen tool to add the veins of the leaf (or any details you desire), also in black. To create disconnected line segments, like the veins, click to add the endpoint and then hit the esc key to end the line and deselect the shape (so you can continue to the next one). When you have the outline design you like, select all of the pieces (click and drag a box around all of the shapes) and "Group" the design by choosing the menu item object and then group. This will make it easy to move around all of the pieces as one unit; note that to select an object with no fill color in Adobe Illustrator, such as this leaf shape, you must click on the outline.

4 **Create the repeat.**
You now have the two basic elements of the design. Copy the outline leaf and paste it onto your design area and move the original solid-colored leaf to align with it; group the two together as in Step 3. Now copy and paste each of the two different leaf designs to create your repeat. Allison's repeat featured two rows of outline leaves alternating with one row of colored leaves, as shown in the photo at left.

5 **Crop, save, and upload.**
Crop your repeat tile, remembering to test and check the alignment if you are making a seamless design (page 62). Save the file, export as a .jpg, and upload it to Spoonflower (page 18). Choose the amount of wallpaper you need and a basic repeat.

installing the table wrap

6 **Measure and trim the wallpaper.**
Using the flexible tape measure, measure the top of your table or the specific area of the table you wish to decorate; we installed a single width of wallpaper around the center of the table. Add several inches (cm) to your measurement to wrap each end to the underside of the table. Cut a piece of wallpaper to match your measurement.

7 **Prepare the surface.**
The surface to which you are applying wallpaper should be clean and free of dust. Patch or sand any rough spots that might tear the paper.

8 Apply the wallpaper.

On the underside of the tabletop, draw a straight line about 3 inches (7.5 cm) from the top, using a ruler or level as needed; peel back 1 to 2 inches (2.5 to 5 cm) of the backing paper from the top of the wallpaper strip and place it on the line. Press it to hold in place. Peel away the backing paper as you wrap the wallpaper over the edge and around to the top of the table. Smooth in place, working from the center out, and wrap the remaining end of the strip to the underside of the table. You can use the edge of a credit card or a rubber squeegee to burnish the paper to the surface and help gently push out any bubbles or wrinkles. Peel-and-stick wallpaper is removable and repositionable, so you should be able to adjust it easily.

If you're interested in using a design like this one to cover your walls, refer to "Wallpaper FYI" on page 126 for information about hanging.

BELOW Papers on the shelves shown designed by (top to bottom): Top two Holli Zollinger, Sarah Walden, Vivian Ducas.

MORE IDEAS

+ Print the same design on fabric to use for other decorating purposes. Make coordinating curtains or pillows, make a duvet cover, or print the design onto heavyweight fabric such as twill or canvas to upholster a chair or an ottoman or even line a bulletin board.

+ If you have leftover wallpaper, think small: check out "A Square Isn't Just a Square" on page 37 to use the remnants to cover notebooks or switch plates, to make bookmarks or gift tags, and so on.

+ Use peel-and-stick wallpaper to inexpensively perk up thrift store finds or any piece of furniture that needs refreshing. Try it on coffee tables, work tables, or dressers. Or use it to line shelves (see left) and drawers.

Risky Business Pouch

AMY PEPPLER ADAMS / SEATTLE, WA

Amy Peppler Adams started designing with Spoonflower in 2010, after a friend told her about the site. The first design she uploaded was an entry in a Tea Towel Calendar challenge, and when it came in second place, she was hooked. Amy—or pennycandy as she is known on the site—earned a degree in graphic design many years ago, before computers were commonplace, then learned digital design on her own. Her wonderful sense of humor comes out in her vibrant, lighthearted work.

MATERIALS & TOOLS

TO DESIGN THE FABRIC

A photo of sunglasses or other object to trace (see Note)

Vector-based graphics program

1 fat quarter of faux suede, canvas, or twill, 27 x 18 inches (68.6 x 46 cm) (we used faux suede)

TO MAKE THE POUCH

Printed fabric

Lining fabric, 27 x 18 inches (68.6 x 46 cm)

10-inch (25.4 cm) chunky coat zipper

Basic sewing tools (page 23)

Rotary cutter, self-healing cutting mat, and acrylic quilter's ruler

Washable fabric-marking pen or chalk

Chopstick, knitting needle, or point turner

Small split ring (optional)

Note: When choosing a subject for your photo, note that you will be tracing the subject, and therefore it will be helpful if you can clearly see it and if there is some contrast between the subject and the background. For a very clean graphic look like Amy's, photograph an item that doesn't have too many details and shoot straight onto it, not from an angle.

designing the fabric

1 Create a new canvas.

Review the information about vector-based images on pages 160–161. Create a canvas that is a several times larger than the design you want to create. Create the shapes you need using the Pen tool; think about breaking up your design into several simple shapes that you can stack or put together. For example, the frames in this design are one solid shape with the lenses arranged on top. Click and place pins anywhere the line needs to change direction. Remember to use the handles as explained on page 160 to adjust the curves and points for each shape. (Alternatively, if you're not confident with your drawing skills, you can trace a photo of an object like we show in the Pet Silhouette Hankies instructions on page 176.)

2 Trace the subject of the photo.

Trace the entire image in your photo using the Pen tool. Click and place pins anywhere the line needs to change direction. Remember to use the handles as explained on page 161 to adjust the curves to match the shape you're tracing. Trace around the lenses separately as you will manipulate them separately in Step 2. The frames in this design are one solid shape with the lenses arranged on top.

When you have the shape complete and adjusted to your liking, select the temporary layer with the photo and delete it.

3 Add colors.

To add the background color, draw a rectangle, fill it with the color black (or the color of your choice), and place it behind the other elements. To color the rest of the image, select the sunglasses frame and choose white (or the color of your

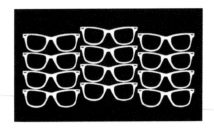

FIGURE 1 To create a seamless tile, first paste multiple copies of your image onto your canvas.

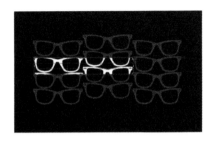

FIGURE 2 The "sparkle" on the left corner of the glasses is the guide element for cropping the art to create the seamless tile.

FIGURE 3 In the top screenshot the rectangle around the sunglass motif contains the entire design without overlapping any other motifs. In the bottom screen shot, the sunglass motifs are closer together; as a result, there is an overlap at the right side of the rectangle with the adjacent motif. This tells you that to make the design work as an uninterrupted pattern, you would need to create a seamless tile.

choice); select the lenses and choose black (or the color you chose for the background).

4 Make the repeat tile.

Many vector programs will let you select a collection of shapes and group them together so you can move them as one object. To do this, first select all of the pieces of your sunglasses and look for a menu item labeled "Group." (You can "Ungroup" if you need to adjust something later.)

If you want to reduce the size of your grouped artwork, do so now (the sunglasses in Amy's fabric are roughly 2 inches (5 cm) wide).

Although this design looks like a simple half-drop repeat that you might choose after you upload a design to Spoonflower, it actually requires a little more finessing because it is seamless. To create a seamless tile, select, copy, and paste multiple copies of your image into a new file, arranging them in a half-drop pattern (Figure 1). Place them very close to each other. Carefully align the motifs so the rows and columns are precise.

Look for a distinctive element in your design or guide element like the "sparkle" at the left corner of the glasses frame. Crop the image, placing the four corners of the crop selection at exactly the same place in relation to the guide element (Figure 2). Remember that some vector-

Do I Want a Seamless Repeat?

For this project, Amy needed to create a seamless repeat from her design to get the sunglasses scrunched up against one another. If you're planning a design and are not sure if you need to take the extra steps to create a seamless repeat, here's a simple trick to help. Mock up your intended pattern of repeats on a scrap of paper or in a blank digital canvas and draw a rectangle around one single motif (Figure 3). Every part of that motif should fit inside the rectangle. If parts of adjoining motifs are also in the rectangle, or the rectangle touches part of the motif itself, then you need to build and crop a seamless tile to achieve an uninterrupted pattern. (You can go old-school and simply trace

around one motif with your fingertip, too, and if you don't touch any part of the design, you don't need to create a seamless repeat).

If you have a newer version of Adobe Illustrator, there is a great pattern-making tool you can explore that has many options for the style of repeat. It also has tools for adjusting the spacing and other variables needed to create a seamless tile. To use it, select the motif and then choose "Create Pattern." Once you have adjusted your pattern, it will be saved and you can use it to fill other shapes; for example, you could use the sunglasses pattern to fill giant polka dots or other shapes.

based graphics programs use artboards instead of the Crop tool; if you're working in such a program, create a new artboard the size of your crop and when you export your artwork as a .jpg, the program will automatically crop the design following the edges of the artboard.

Test your repeat as suggested in the Squid Damask Shower Curtain (page 137) and check the edges of your design carefully where they should align; the lines should be smooth. It is easy to be off by a pixel or two, so you might need to undo and re-crop to get your repeat lined up precisely.

making the pouch

5 Save and upload your design.
Save the file, export as a .jpg, and upload it to Spoonflower (page 18). Choose a fat quarter of fabric and a basic repeat.

6 Prepare your fabric.
Wash, dry, and press your outside (printed) and lining fabrics. From each outside and lining fabric, cut 2 squares that are 12½ x 12½ inches (31.8 x 31.8 cm). From the printed fabric only, cut two rectangles that are 1½ x 2 inches (4 x 5 cm) for the zipper ends; if you would like an optional zipper pull, cut a rectangle 1 x 5 inches (2.5 x 12 cm).

7 Stitch the zipper ends.
At each end of the zipper, align one of the small rectangles so that one short edge matches the end of the zipper tape. Use a small backstitch to hand-sew the rectangle to the zipper tape, ½-inch (1.2 cm) from each end, as this zipper is bulky and impossible to sew on a machine. Fold the fabric to the outside along the stitching line and press. Trim any extra zipper tape.

8 Install the zipper.
Place one square of lining fabric right side up. Center the zipper on the top edge of the square of fabric, right side up, aligning the long edge of the tape with the edge of the lining. Place one square of outside fabric right side down and align with the top edge of the lining and the zipper. Pin in place. Install a zipper foot on your sewing machine and stitch across the top edge through all layers, close to the zipper teeth. Open out the fabric layers, fold them back along the stitching line, and press. Repeat these steps to stitch the opposite side of the zipper tape. Trim the extra fabric from the zipper ends.

9 Stitch the outside seam.

Unzip the zipper. Fold the bag in half with the right sides of the printed fabric facing each other on the inside and the right sides of the lining pieces covering them, facing the outside. Match and pin the sides and bottom edges. Stitch around the sides and bottom of the bag using a ½-inch (1.2 cm) seam allowance. Reinforce and finish the edge by stitching again with a wide zigzag stitch (or use a serger if you have one).

10 Stitch the gussets.

Open out one bottom corner of the bag and press it flat, matching the seamlines from the side and bottom. Pin. Measure 2 inches (5 cm) from that corner and use the fabric marker to draw a line perpendicular to the seamlines. Using a straight stitch, stitch through all layers, following the marked line. Trim away the extra fabric at the corner, leaving about a ¼-inch (6 mm) seam allowance (Figure 4). Finish with a zigzag stitch or a serger. Repeat for the other corner.

11 Turn and press.

Turn the bag right side out and use a chopstick, point turner, or knitting needle to press out the corners at the bottom and at the zipper ends. Press.

12 Add an optional zipper pull.

To add a zipper pull, fold the long edges of the 1 x 5-inch (2.5 x 12 cm) fabric rectangle to meet in the center and press. Fold again in half, matching the long edges. Stitch close to the folded edges. Trim the short ends at an angle. Thread the zipper pull through a small split ring and fold in half. Stitch across the fabric close to the ring and backstitch to reinforce. Slip the split ring onto the zipper pull.

MORE IDEAS

+ To coordinate your lining fabric with the main pouch fabric, use the color tools explained on pages 114–115.

+ Interested in using a different subject matter for your photo? Here are a few ideas: landmarks like the Eiffel Tower or the Statue of Liberty; everyday items such as keys, pencils, or clothespins; cosmetic products like lipsticks, combs, or brushes; or classic automobiles or vintage motorcycles. You can use copyright-free clip art as the subject for your drawing, too.

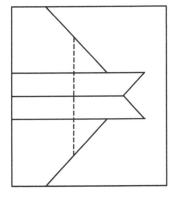

DRAW A LINE PERPENDICULAR
TO THE SEAM. STITCH ON THE LINE.

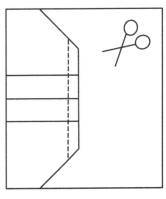

TRIM

FIGURE 4 Stitching the gussets (Step 10).

Fabric pouches are irresistible to a lot of us, especially when we have so much special fabric around. Here we used two of Holli Zollinger's prints to make pouches similar to the one on page 170. We changed the shape to a rectangle and followed Steps 6 through 11 minus the gussets. You can make these simple bags in virtually any size or shape you want so long as you have a zipper that fits along the top edge.

Pet Silhouette Hankies

Sharing pet photos is up there with sharing baby photos—no matter what, it's hard to resist. For these hankies, we used photos of our dear canine and feline friends—Frank, Jack Sparrow, Toshi, and Maggie Mae—to create silhouettes that we used instead of traditional monograms on cotton hankies.

designing the fabric

MATERIALS & TOOLS

TO DESIGN THE FABRIC
A pet photo (see Note)
Vector-based graphics
  program
1 yard (.9 m) of basic cotton,
  sateen, or silk crepe de
  chine (we used basic
  cotton)

TO MAKE THE HANKIE
Printed fabric
Basic sewing tools (page 23)

Note: It's best to use a photo of your pet by him or herself, with nothing in front of your pet's image. We gave tips about photographing your pet in the Doppelganger Dog Pillow project on page 105, and each of them also apply to this project; pay particular attention to the tip about capturing your pet's unique characteristics so you can create a singular silhouette.

1 **Create a new canvas.**
Review the information about vector-based images on pages 160–161. This technique uses a photograph as the basis for your design, so create a canvas that is a several times larger than the original photo you will use. Place or insert the photo you will trace into the canvas. This layer will be temporary; you will use it to help trace the shapes you need and then it will be removed later.

2 **Trace your pet.**
Using the Pen tool, trace around the outline of your pet, clicking and placing pins where the line needs to change direction. Remember to use the handles (page 161) to adjust the curves to match the shape of your pet. When you have completed the shape and adjusted it to your liking, you can select the temporary photo layer and delete it.

3 **Create a new file and add the background.**
Create a new file for the hankie, 12 x 12 inches (30.5 x 30.5 cm) / 1800 x 1800 pixels. Draw a square that fills the entire canvas for the background layer of the hankie. Fill it with a color; we made a variety of hankies from diverse pet silhouettes and made each of the backgrounds a different color—pink, green, yellow, and blue.

4 **Add a border and circles.**
Many vector programs have tools or functions that will automatically make basic shapes like squares and circles. Use this tool to add a 10-inch (25.4 cm) square for the border of the design; you can also use the Pen tool to draw a square. Center the square in the canvas. Fill it with the same color you chose for your background in Step 3 and add an outline in a contrasting color (we used white). To make the circles, use the shapes tool again to create circles and place them inside the square shape, using the same colors to fill and

MAGGIE MAE

FRANK

JACK SPARROW

TOSHI

outline them as you used to make the square. Some programs will let you add an effect like a dotted or dashed line to the outline of your shape; we used this option in our project.

5 **Place your silhouette and personalize.**
Copy and paste your pet shape into the hankie design. Choose a contrasting color (we used gray) and fill the pet shape. Click and drag at the corners of the shape to adjust the size of your silhouette and place it in the lower right-hand corner of the hankie. Use the Text tool to add your pet's name; we used dark grey text.

6 **Save and upload.**
Save the file, export as a .jpg, and upload it to Spoonflower (page 18). Choose a lightweight fabric and repeat the design to fill as much fabric as you like; you can get 9 hankies from 1 yard (.9 m) of basic cotton.

making the hankie

7 **Cut out the fabric.**
Wash and press your fabric. Carefully cut out the hankies. Having nice, even edges will make rolling the hems easier and will look tidier, too. Once they're all cut apart, press the hankies again if needed.

8 **Make a rolled hem.**
Thread a sharp needle with a single length of coordinating thread and knot the end. With the hankie facing wrong side up, start at a top corner and roll the edge toward you, using your thumb and forefinger. The hem roll should take up about ¼ inch (6 mm) of fabric. Make the roll nice and tight so that the raw edges of the fabric are securely enclosed.

Insert the threaded needle through the end of the rolled tube and bring it out about ½ inch (1.2 cm) away from the corner and near the bottom edge of the roll. Take a tiny stitch in the hankie fabric, picking up just a couple of threads. Insert the needle again into the bottom edge of the roll and bring the needle back out again ¼ inch (6 mm) away. Once again, take a tiny stitch that picks up just a couple of threads on the hankie. Continue on in this way until you're close to the first corner.

As you near the first corner, roll the next side of the hankie to meet the first side, rolling evenly from both sides so that you maintain as much of a crisp point as possible. You should end up with a wee mitered corner.

Continue on in this way until you've hemmed the entire hankie.

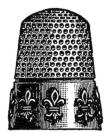

ABOVE The clip art Caroline used to create the thimble and spool of thread pillows at right came from pixgood. com and thegraphicsfairy.com, respectively. Using a special Illustrator tool called Image Trace, she was able to convert the original raster images into vector format and enlarge them.

We take these Sewing Notions Pillows designed by Spoonflower art director Caroline Okun to trade shows, and they always attract a lot of attention. Although they don't look at all like the Pet Silhouette Hankies, they're actually based on a similar concept: tracing artwork (pet photos for the hankies, copyright-free vintage illustrations for the pillows). The difference is that for the hankies, you trace with the Pen tool, and for the pillows you trace with an Illustrator tool called Image Trace. This tool converts raster images to vector format so you can enlarge and modify them. The Image Trace tool is complex; the instructions here are specific to working with a black-and-white illustration.

Start with a canvas slightly bigger than your desired project size, leaving room for a ½-inch (1.2 cm) seam allowance and some blank fabric to frame the illustration. Choose "Place" under the "File" menu to add the illustration to the canvas. (If you need to resize your image, click it with the Direct Select tool now.)

Under the "Window" menu, choose "Image Trace" to open the tool panel. Be sure the "default" preset is chosen so the illustration remains black and white; also check "Ignore White" under the Advanced options. Choose "Trace" to create a vector image preview. Click "Expand" in the Image Trace control panel, and

switch to RBG mode in the Color Palette so you can change the black by clicking on your desired color.

Choose "Deselect" from the Select menu and create a new layer. Working on this new layer—not the original illustration layer—use the Pen tool to trace the parts of the image you want to fill with another color. Use the Direct Select tool to refine your selection by adjusting the points as needed (page 161). When you're satisfied with your tracing done with the Pen, you can rearrange so the original illustration layer is on top. Add more color as desired.

Save the design and export as a .jpg to upload to Spoonflower. Depending on design size, print on a fat quarter or 1 yard (.9 m) of fabric. You'll also need the same amount of fabric to make the pillow back, plus stuffing. Follow Steps 5 and 6 on page 107 to sew a pillow.

Notes: Depending on the version of Illustrator, commands may be slightly different than those here. In versions earlier than CS6, use a similar tool called Live Trace, then use the Pen tool to refine the design. For free, vintage, copyright-free illustrations, check antiqueimages.blogspot.com, oldbookillustrations.com, pixgood.com, and thegraphicsfairy.com.

THE WORLD OF VECTORS

11

NO REPEATS NECESSARY
Design Cut & Sew and Whole Cloth

OPPOSITE A map of a
favorite city inspired these
pillowcases.

Many of the projects we've presented so far have been based on repeat patterns. But you can also create patterns that don't repeat or that only repeat to fill part of a space. This technique is called "whole cloth" design or "whole surface" design, because your design takes up the entirety of what you are printing, without repeating.

These designs often are created as separate elements and then combined together into one file. The finished design could fit on a fat quarter . . . or it could fit on 2 yards (2 m) of fabric. It's your choice!

You may not have noticed at the time, but the Flutter Baby Quilt (page 121) is an example of a whole cloth design, because the entire yard (.9 m) of fabric is filled with one large image. You also may have heard of cut-and-sew projects, where all of the pattern pieces for a project such as a soft toy are grouped together on a single piece of fabric. Then they are printed, cut out, and sewn.

There is so much you can do with whole surface or cut-and-sew designs. Projects we commonly see at Spoonflower include:

+ Stuffed toys and dolls, like the Gnome Stuffed Toy on page 184

+ Clothing, such as skirts; kids' shirts or dresses; or accessories such as bags and purses with relatively few pattern pieces—the Stacked Skeins Skirt on page 193 is an example of a cut-and-sew garment

+ Quilt tops (called "cheater quilts" because they mimic the look of real patchwork)

Choose Your Surface First

The first thing to think about when you are creating a whole surface design is what surface you want to fill, of course. If you need a refresher course on how to choose a surface, flip back to page 34. Only when you know the size of the surface can you set up your file to create a design that fits exactly on it.

Let's use the cut-and-sew Gnome Stuffed Toy on page 184 as an example. Let's pretend you are designing it and you would like to fit the pattern pieces on a fat quarter of twill that is 29 x 18 inches (73.7 x 46 cm). Your new canvas for a fat quarter will need to be 4350 x 2700 pixels (Figure 1), based on the Pixel Equation (page 42):

29 INCHES X 150 DPI = 4350 PIXELS

18 INCHES X 150 DPI = 2700 PIXELS

Now you can lay out all of the pieces to see if they fit on the digital canvas and if they do, you know that they will fit on your printed surface. If they don't fit, then you know you need to revise the size or scale of your design.

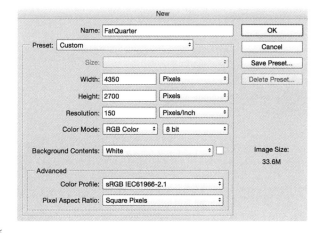

FIGURE 1 To create a whole surface design, first you need to set up a file that matches the size of your desired surface. The file here is set up for a fat quarter of our twill, which is 29 x 18 inches (73.7 x 46 cm) / 4350 x 2700 pixels at 150 dpi.

Rulers and Grid View

When you are working with a specific-size design or a cut-and-sew project with multiple pattern pieces, it's helpful to be able to tell at a glance how large a piece is or how much space you have between the pieces. Since it's very hard to determine spacing and scale by looking at your computer screen, many programs have an option that allows you to view rulers and/or a grid in the design space.

Rulers are visible along the sides of your canvas, much like the rulers you see when you upload your designs to Spoonflower. The option to turn on rulers is generally under the "View" menu (Figure 2). You can also turn on a grid, a transparent set of lines (like graph paper) that appear under your image while you work. You can usually set the distance of the grid markings to your preferred scale

(i.e., 1 inch [2.5 cm] apart or ¼ inch [6 mm] apart). Look for a menu option that says "Show Grid" to turn it on (Figure 3).

One additional function we use in this chapter is the guideline, a highlighted line in your canvas that helps you line up elements easily or place points to create a shape to specific dimensions. The guideline function is only available in Adobe Photoshop or Illustrator, and it does not have an icon or symbol. (You can use a ruler or grid in another program to help you align elements.) To make a guideline in either Photoshop or Illustrator, click inside the top or left ruler area and drag into the page. You will see a colored guideline appear (Figure 4). To move a guideline after you have placed it, switch to the Select tool, click on the guideline, and drag it.

Tips for Whole Cloth and Cut & Sew Projects

+ Place pattern pieces so you have room for seam allowances. Use the grid/rulers to check, and also review the sidebar on page 186 to learn how to add seam allowances easily in Illustrator.

+ When working with fabric, think about the way your pieces are arranged on the fabric and the direction of the fabric grain. Remember pieces placed on the diagonal/bias will stretch (page 31).

+ Surfaces at Spoonflower are printed following the crosswise grain of the material (page 31). If you want your finished pieces to go perpendicular to the grain, then rotate 90° or set up your file to match. This technique is used in the World Traveler Pillowcase (page 189).

FIGURE 2 Turn on the ruler function to help judge spacing and scale.

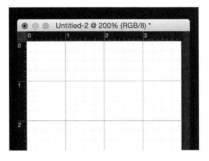

FIGURE 3 The grid also helps to judge spacing and scale; you can usually customize the distance of the grid markings.

FIGURE 4 Use guidelines (shown in blue here) to line up elements or place points.

NO REPEATS NECESSARY

Gnome Stuffed Toy

JOCELAN THIESSEN / VANCOUVER, BRITISH COLUMBIA

A Vancouver-based storyboard artist for cartoons, Jocelan Thiessen (cutesypoo on Spoonflower) loves making 3-D representations of her sketches. For this gnome, she wanted something modern and simple: the easiest toy possible without compromising appeal. It was her first foray into using Spoonflower, and she was instantly hooked! Her husband, Jayson, pitched in to help take this charming fellow from doodle to doll by re-creating Jocelan's hand-drawn sketch in a vector program.

designing the fabric

MATERIALS & TOOLS

TO DESIGN THE FABRIC

Paper and drawing media of your choice and/or vector-based graphics program

1 fat quarter of twill, 29 x 18 inches (73.7 x 46 cm) (see Note for other fabric choices)

TO MAKE THE GNOME

Printed fabric

Basic sewing tools (page 23)

Chopstick, knitting needle, or point turner

Polyfill or other stuffing

Plastic bean-bag pellets (optional)

Note: While sateen, canvas, basic cotton, and even knit fabrics could be appropriate for this project, each of them has a different width, and thus their fat quarters are different sizes. Be sure to set up your canvas for the correct size if you use a fabric other than twill, and note the information about scaling a design in Step 3.

1 Create a new canvas and turn on rulers.

Create a new canvas that is sized for a fat quarter of your chosen fabric. This toy is made from heavy twill, so Jocelan created a file that is 29 x 18 inches (73.7 x 46 cm) / 4350 x 2700 pixels. Turn on the grid view (if available) and rulers to help place the pieces you create in Step 2, especially if you want to place them along the straight grain of the fabric—more about this in Step 3.

2 Create the parts of your toy.

Review the information about whole cloth and cut-and-sew designs on pages 182–183. Using the shapes or Pen tool in your program, make two circles: a circle for the base that is 6 inches (15 cm) in diameter and a large circle that is 24 inches (61 cm) in diameter. With the large 24-inch circle, draw a cone for the body that is a quarter of a circle. Think of it like a big piece of pie! Your "piece of pie" will have 12-inch (30.5 cm) straight sides when cut from a larger circle.

Now add color and design to the two pattern pieces. Make the base a solid color and draw clothing and facial features onto the cone-shaped body piece (or create your own version of this simple toy—you could make yours more like an animal than a human or you could just stick with this shape and add a less literal, more decorative design, for example). For the body, use some of the shapes available in your graphics program to create various parts, such as a circle or ellipse shape for the eyes and a rectangle for the belt buckle (use a Line tool to make the belt itself). You could also use the Pen tool to make all the shapes, including additional facial features. Fill each area with color; remember that you can layer shapes and move them forward or backward as needed to create backgrounds, such as the swirls for the hat and the checks for the clothing.

3 Arrange your pieces.

Use the grids/rulers to double-check the size of each piece to make sure you sized your pieces as instructed in Step 1 and have enough room for seam allowances. Remember that if you decide to scale a piece up or down, you will want to make the same change to each of the pieces so that they will fit together when you are ready to sew. Arrange each piece leaving at least a ¼-inch (6 mm) seam allowance around all sides of the shape moving them as needed (Figure 1). You can rotate pieces to fit them in the space, but think about the fabric grain (page 31) as you do this. The rulers or guides can give you an easy reference to check to see if your pieces are aligned properly, since the lines can represent the lengthwise or crosswise grain of the fabric.

4 Save and upload.

Save the file and upload it to Spoonflower (page 18). Select a fat quarter of your chosen fabric and a centered repeat.

FIGURE 1 Place your shapes to make sure they fit into the canvas.

Adding A "Digital" Seam Allowance

For many projects, you can just add the seam allowance when you cut out your shapes. But if you want to have a printed seam allowance line for a cut-and-sew project—and eliminate the threat of forgetting to include a seam allowance when cutting—you can add it in just a few steps if you have Adobe Illustrator. Use the Select tool to click and select the entire vector shape. Look in the menu for the option "Object," then choose "Path," and then choose "Offset Path" (Figure 2).

A box will pop up with some options. Type in the desired seam allowance. For example, ".5 in" will add ½ inch (1.2 cm) all around your shape (Figure 3). You can fill this new shape with a color or use the outline as the new cutting line for the shape.

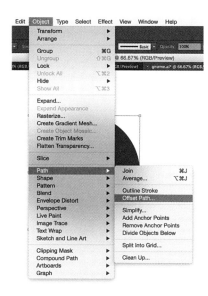

FIGURE 2 To add a seam allowance in Illustrator, first select the entire vector shape, then choose "Path" and "Offset Path" in the Object menu.

FIGURE 3 Then type in the desired seam allowance (here it is .5 in).

making the gnome

5 Cut out the pieces.

Cut out the pieces of your gnome. Make sure you include ¼ inch (6 mm) around all sides for the seam allowance.

6 Pin and stitch the body.

Fold the body in half with right sides together, matching the long straight sides. Pin and stitch together, leaving a 2-inch (5 cm) opening in the center to use for turning the toy right side out. Leave the body inside-out for now.

7 Add the base.

Pin the base to the bottom edge of the body with the right sides facing. Stitch around the outside edge using a ¼-inch (6 mm) seam allowance.

8 Clip, turn, and stuff.

Clip the curves around the base. Trim the seam allowance slightly at the point of the cone. Turn your gnome right side out. Stuff firmly, starting at the tip of the cone and working down. Use a chopstick or knitting needle to help stuff the small space at the tip. As you get to the bottom of the toy, you can add some bean-bag pellets to give your toy some weight to stand up on its own. Slipstitch the opening.

MORE IDEAS

+ Rather than creating your toy in a vector-based program, you can also draw your toy pieces entirely by hand and scan them, then place them into a graphics program for layout. Choose the scan settings based on the largest piece and the size you want it to be when finished. For example, if you want the body of the toy to be about 12 inches (30.5 cm) tall, similar to the gnome, then you would scan it at a minimum of 12 inches x 150 ppi = 1800 pixels. Make sure that you scan all of your pieces at the same settings so they maintain their proportions and will fit together when sewn.

+ This shape can be interpreted in lots of fun ways. What about a set of really awesome bowling pins? Or some upside-down ice cream cones, just for giggles? Several of these toys, in the same or varying sizes, could make an interesting collection of soft sculpture.

World Traveler Pillowcase

STACY IEST HSU / SAN CARLOS, CA

Being a mom to three young kids is a full-time job for Stacy Iest Hsu, who started designing on Spoonflower (as stacyiesthsu) after her own mother told her about it. Stacy's first design was for a contest about outer space designs, and that experience was all she needed to get hooked (that, and her Wacom tablet).

Stacy designed this Berlin map–inspired fabric to celebrate her love for exploring new countries. Her passport hasn't seen much activity lately, but she suspects new adventures are on the horizon, with three new explorers ready to go.

designing the fabric

MATERIALS & TOOLS

TO DESIGN THE FABRIC

A vector design program or digital drawing tablet

1 yard (.9 m) of basic cotton or sateen (we used basic cotton)

TO MAKE THE PILLOWCASE

Printed fabric

Basic sewing tools (page 23)

1 Create the pillowcase repeat.

Review the information about whole cloth and cut-and-sew designs on pages 182–183. This pillowcase has two different repeat patterns, a main design for the body of the pillowcase and a coordinate for the hem.

Make a map design by following the same process we used for the Pet Silhouette Hankies (page 176), tracing over an actual map (rather than a photo of your pet). Get a map of your favorite place by scanning a paper copy, finding an image online (Google Maps is a good source) and downloading it, or by taking a screenshot. Place that image into your design file, trace over it using vector lines, and then delete the actual map layer when you are done. Some additional tips:

+ Don't try to trace every road and detail, but look for the main streets and those that might make interesting or distinctive shapes.

+ It is easier to use maps that have a basic grid shape with some interesting road patterns. Maps with a lot of curved roads can sometimes be challenging because it is hard to match the repeat nicely.

+ Add rivers, lakes, or other features in a contrasting color.

If you want to make a seamless repeat for this design (which we have to admit is a little tricky), once you have laid out your main features, crop to create your repeat tile (page 164). To make the roads, rivers, or other features that meet at the edges of the repeat match up, check that the line ending at the right edge of the design has a line to match it starting at the left edge. If they don't match up, change the lines you traced by altering their pin points or curves (page 161). This may take a little patience and some trial and error as you check the crop to make sure it works. Review the information about seamless repeats on pages 62–63.

2 Create the hem repeat.

The coordinating pattern for the hem section of the pillowcase can be anything that complements the design. (See the sidebar at right for some hints about creating coordinates.) For this map design, Stacy created an eccentric polka dot from little circles, which reminds us of lights in buildings at night, and made a chevron pattern from thin slanted rectangles, which complements the lines in the map and might bring to mind traffic signals or street signs. She matched the colors in the hem design to those used in the body design. As we explained in "Making a Repeat Pattern in Photoshop" on page 138, you can save these patterns and use them to fill the shapes you make in Step 3.

Note: The layout of this design is perpendicular to the grain of the fabric. In other words, the repeats should be rotated 90° so the designs are oriented with the length of the fabric when printed (pages 149–150).

3 Lay out the pillowcase.

Create a new file that is the size of the whole cloth you want to print. For this pillowcase, you want 1 yard (.9 m) of fabric 42 x 36 inches (107 x 91 cm) / 6300 x 5400 pixels. Turn on the rulers/grid view.

The pillowcase design is made up of three basic rectangles side by side (Figure 1).

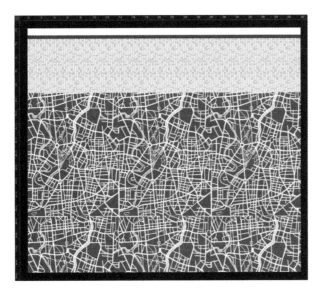

FIGURE 1 The pillowcase file is divided into three sections, shown here top to bottom: hem allowance, hem, and body.

+ For the hem allowance, make a rectangle that is 42 x ½ inches (107 x 1.2 cm). Fill it with a solid color; this area won't show after the pillowcase is sewn.

+ For the hem, make a rectangle that is 42 x 8 inches (107 x 20 cm). Fill it with the coordinating repeat pattern. Use a pattern fill as referenced in Step 2 or simply copy and paste the tile to fill the space. When you sew the pillowcase, this hem section will be folded in half, so 4 inches (10 cm) of this rectangle will show on the outside of the pillowcase and 4 inches (10 cm) will be on the inside.

+ For the body of the pillowcase, make a rectangle that is 42 x 26½ inches (107 x 67.3 cm). Fill this rectangle with the main pillowcase repeat pattern. The body will be folded in half lengthwise when it is stitched. There will be 1 inch (2.5 cm) of unprinted space at the edge of your design.

4 Save and upload.

Save the file and upload it to Spoonflower (page 18). Choose a centered repeat and 1 yard (.9 m) of fabric.

making the pillowcase

5 Trim, press, and hem.

Trim away the selvedges and the excess inch (2.5 cm) of fabric. Place the fabric wrong side up. Turn the hem allowance ½ inch (1.2 cm) toward the inside and press. Fold the hem in half, 4 inches (10 cm) toward the inside of the fabric, and press. Pin the hem in place. Stitch close to the inside fold.

6 Make a French seam.

Fold the pillowcase in half lengthwise, wrong sides together. Pin and stitch the long sides using a ¼-inch (6 mm) seam allowance. Trim the seam allowance slightly. Turn inside out, so the right sides are together, and press. Stitch again with a ¼ inch (6 mm) seam allowance, encasing the raw edges inside the new seam allowance.

7 Stitch the end.

Stitch the end of the pillowcase, using a ½ inch (1.2 cm) seam allowance. Turn right side out and press.

Creating Coordinates

Coordinates are a set of complementary fabrics that share some common characteristics, such as color or motifs, so they can be used together harmoniously. Stacy used two coordinating prints for the hems of these pillowcases. There are many opinions about what makes good coordinates, but here are a few ideas to consider.

COLOR: If you are designing a print to complement a multicolored pattern, you might consider designing one that reads as a solid even if it has a pattern, perhaps with a small-scale print. Use a color from the main print that is not dominant, so when you place the designs next to each other, there is visual interest created by the complementary contrast between them.

SCALE: The main pattern in a collection of fabrics is usually larger than the other designs in scale. By designing coordinates slightly smaller in scale, they are less likely to overpower the main print.

REPEAT DESIGN ELEMENTS: A popular trick for creating coordinates is pulling small elements from the main print. For instance, if your design features large flowers surrounded by smaller flowers, the smaller flowers can be the basis for a coordinating pattern. Geometric prints, stripes, and polka dots are wonderful for coordinates because they can complement any fabric design.

Stacked Skeins Skirt

BECKA RAHN / MINNEAPOLIS, MN

Becka Rahn loves to design fabric for clothing (check out her Infinity Scarf on page 92), because of the way she can deliberately place patterns for maximum effect. She especially likes to manipulate photos so they become more abstract and textural, like this skirt fabric she designed using a photo of the much-admired wall-of-yarn at the Weavers Guild of Minnesota. Her collection of photography is her favorite digital design tool because it inspires so many of her ideas.

The grand finale for our book is divided into three sections. The design is in two parts: first, you will learn to draft a simple A-line skirt to fit your measurements, and second, you will manipulate the photo to create the fabric design. The third part is simple cut-and-sew instructions to make the skirt. You will get to use many of the skills learned throughout the book, as well as try out some new tools in Adobe Photoshop and Illustrator; because of the complex nature of this project, you can only create it using these graphics programs in combination.

Note: Because the pieces for this skirt are designed for an exact fit, you must consider your fabric's expected rate of shrinkage when you are creating this design; shrinkage information is provided on the website. To accommodate the widest range of fabrics and to give you more freedom to choose which type of fabric you prefer—crisp canvas or cotton with more structure or silky faille with a lot of drape—we've written basic instructions that you can tailor to your fabric. If you choose linen-cotton canvas or sateen, add 1 inch (2.5 cm) to your length measurement and an additional ¼ inch (6 mm) to your seam allowances when you create your design to account for shrinkage; you can fine-tune your fit as you sew. Silky faille will not shrink, so you can follow the instructions exactly as presented here.

drafting the skirt pattern

1 Take your measurements.

You need four basic measurements to make an A-line skirt: waist, hips, rise, and length; see below for more details. The more accurately you measure, the better the fit. Don't measure over your regular clothes. Put on something close fitting such as a leotard and tights and get a friend to help so you can measure accurately. You'll be marking spots directly on these garments.

WAIST: Measure where you want the finished waistline to fall, which is not necessarily at your natural waist. Pull the measuring tape snug but not tight. Write down this measurement to the closest ⅛ inch (3 mm). Use a piece of masking tape or a pin to mark on your garment where you measured this waistline height. You will need this mark for a later step.

MATERIALS & TOOLS

TO DRAFT THE PATTERN

Adobe Illustrator
Flexible measuring tape
A few pins or pieces of
  masking tape

TO DESIGN THE FABRIC

Adobe Photoshop
A high-quality photograph
  (see sidebar on page 198)
1 to 2 yards (.9 to 2 m) of
  linen-cotton canvas, silky
  faille, sateen (see Note—
  Becka used linen-cotton
  canvas)

TO MAKE THE SKIRT

Printed fabric
7- or 9-inch (17.5 or 23 cm)
  zipper
Seam ripper
1 package of single-fold
  ½-inch (1.2 cm) bias tape
  in a matching or contrasting
  color
1 small hook-and-eye closure
Basic sewing tools (page 23)

HIPS: Measure at the widest part of your bum. Mark this hipline height on your garment with another piece of masking tape or a pin.

RISE: This is the distance between your hips and your waist, which is the measurement in inches (cm) between the two marked spots.

LENGTH: Measure the total length you want the skirt to be, from the waistline to the hem. See Note on page 193 about shrinkage.

Now you need to do a little math to transform these measurements into numbers to use for patternmaking.

+ **WAIST (W):** You will probably want to add some ease to the waistline of your pattern—ease is the amount of extra room you like in the fit of your clothes. For a waistline, you usually want to add up to ½ inch (1.2 cm) to your overall measurement. Then divide this total number by 4, because you will add the ease incrementally to both front and back, right and left sides. (Waist + ease) ÷ 4 = W

+ **HIPS (H):** You will need to add ease to the hips measurement so that you can move and sit down in your skirt comfortably. Add about 1 to 3 inches (2.5 to 7.5 cm) to the hip measurement. Then divide this total number by 4, as was done for the waist measurement. (Hips + ease) ÷ 4 = H

+ Rise (R) and Length (D) measurements are used as is and do not need adjustment.

2 Create a new canvas.

Review the information about whole cloth and cut-and-sew designs on pages 182–183. Make a new canvas in Adobe Illustrator. Create a document that is at least 36 x 36 inches (91 x 91 cm) with plenty of space to work, as you will draft the skirt to scale.

Turn on the rulers and grid view. Adjust the units and spacing on both tools to ¼ inch (6 mm) increments by going to the "Illustrator" menu item, choosing "Preferences," and then choosing "Units." Then go to the "Illustrator" menu item, choose "Preferences," and then choose "Grids & Guides."

Remember, these grids and guides will not show up in the final project, they are just to help draft the pattern.

3 Set up guidelines.

Refer to the measurements you took earlier. Each is labeled W, H, R, and D. Refer to Figure 1 as you work through Step 3.

First, lay out the horizontal guidelines (page 183).

+ Place one guideline at 2 inches (5 cm) from the top of canvas. (1)

+ Place one guideline that is (R) inches (cm) below line 1. (2)

+ Place one more line that is (D) inches (cm) below line 1. (3)

+ Put another guideline ½ inch (1.2 cm) above line 1. (4)

+ Put another guideline 1¼ inches (3.2 cm) above line 3. (5)

Now, lay out the vertical guidelines.

+ Place a guideline in the center of the canvas. (6)

+ Place a guideline that is (W) inches (cm) to the left of the centerline. Add another that is (W) inches (cm) to the right of the centerline. (7)

+ Drop a guideline that is (H) inches (cm) to the left of the centerline. Add another that is (H) inches (cm) to the right of the centerline. (8)

Once the guidelines are inserted, lock them in place so you don't accidentally move them around as you work on the rest of the design. Go to the "View" menu item, choose "Guides," and then choose "Lock Guides."

4 Draw the skirt shape.

See Figures 2 and 3 to make the skirt shape. Start at the top left and continue clockwise around the shape beginning with the waistband curve. At the top left click point W (intersection of lines 4 and 7). Continue the line by clicking the center point (where lines 1 and 6 cross) and dragging to make a curved line. Then click at point W on the right side (the intersection of lines 4 and 7). Don't worry if your curve is not

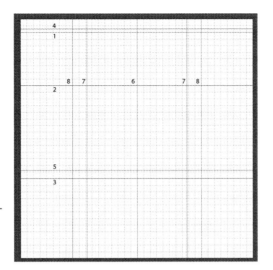

FIGURE 1 Use the Guideline function to place eight guidelines based on your measurements to help you to accurately draft the skirt pattern.

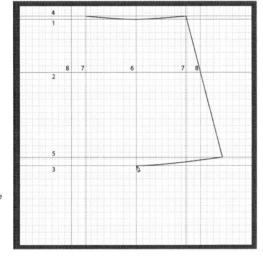

FIGURE 2 Starting at top left of waistband, use the Pen tool to place the points and curves to form the waistband, sides, and hem.

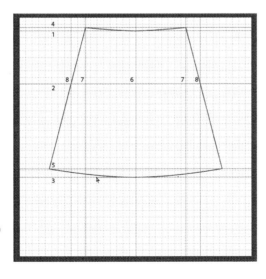

FIGURE 3 Use the Direct Select tool and handles to adjust the curves at the waist and hem so they are smooth and symmetrical.

quite symmetrical as you can go back with the Direct Select tool and adjust it later. This is the waistline.

From point W (intersection of lines 4 and 7) click to create a straight line that crosses point H (intersection of lines 2 and 8) and ends at line 5. To make a straight line, click to create the end point, but don't drag to pull out the handles, just click to make the other end of the line.

Continue the line to draw the curve at the hem by clicking back to the bottom center point (intersection of lines 3 and 6) and dragging to form the curve. Then click to place the lower left corner of the skirt shape. You will need to approximate the placement of this point, making it symmetrical with the right side and go back to adjust later. Finally, close the shape by clicking again to make a straight line ending at the starting point at the top left.

5 **Adjust the curves.**

Use the Direct Select tool to go back and adjust the curves: make sure the curves at the waist and hem are symmetrical and that they form smooth curves from the sides to the center without bulging in or out; adjust the position of the lower corners so that the side seamlines are each crossing point H (intersection of lines 2 and 8) and ending at line 5.

6 Add the seam allowance.

See Note about shrinkage on page 193 before adding seam allowances. Use the Select tool (page 161) to click and select your entire shape. Go to the "Object" menu item and choose "Path," then "Offset Path." In the box labeled "Offset," type in ".5 in" to add a ½-inch (1.2 cm) seam allowance and click OK. A second shape will appear that is ½-inch (1.2 cm) bigger on all sides than the original skirt shape. You can now select and delete that original smaller shape (Figures 4 and 5).

7 Make the waistband facing.

In the toolbar (the collection of available tools), click and hold the Pen tool icon. A menu will pop up with options. Choose the Add Anchor Point tool, which looks like a pen with a + next to it (Figure 6). Click on each side seamline to add an anchor point about 3½ inches (8.9 cm) down the side (Figure 7).

Switch to the Direct Select tool, and hold down the Shift key and click while you select the following points: the two new side seam points you just added and the other points along the top edge of the waistband. Copy and paste this selection to make a duplicate of the top edge of the skirt. Switch back to the Pen tool and connect the bottom

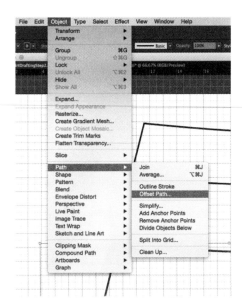

FIGURE 4 Digitally add the seam allowance to your pattern using the Offset Path function.

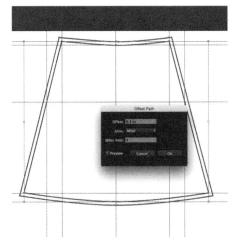

FIGURE 5 In the Offset Path dialog box, enter the seam allowance amount (½ inch [1.2 cm]) to create a new shape that is ½ inch (1.2 cm) larger on all sides.

FIGURE 6 To draw the facing, add a couple of extra points to the side seams using the Add Anchor Point tool (a variation on the Pen tool).

edges of the waistband facing by clicking the points and adjusting the curve (Figure 8).

8 Save and test.

It is a good idea to print this pattern on paper and make a test skirt to adjust any fit issues before you complete your design. You can go back to this file and adjust the measurements as needed. Either print the pattern at home on multiple pieces of paper and tape them together, or see if your local copy shop has a large-format printer and can print for you if you send them a .pdf file or take it to them on a flash drive.

Use some muslin or inexpensive fabric and follow the sewing instructions that follow to baste together the skirt and try it on to make sure you like the fit. Remember, once you have this part of the design finished, you will have a skirt pattern you can use over and over with different surface designs. It is worth the time at this step to get the pattern right!

9 Create a solid shape and save.

Once you have finalized the fit of your pattern, switch to the Select tool. Select and fill the skirt and facing shapes with black and make the outline blank, which is shown with a red line through the box. Save the file (Figure 9).

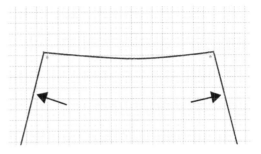

FIGURE 7 The arrows show the placement of the two new points, which are about 3½ inches (8.9 cm) from the waistline.

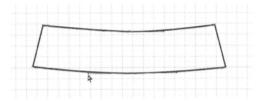

FIGURE 8 To make a facing that exactly matches the top of the skirt, copy and paste the points that form the top of the skirt. Connect the bottom points and adjust the curve.

FIGURE 9 To complete the pattern pieces, fill the skirt and facing shapes with black with no outline.

Choosing a Photo for Your Skirt

Making a great manipulated photo design is all about seeing the potential in a photograph. It doesn't need to be a technically "great" photograph because you are using it as a tool to create a piece of art. (Of course, you can also use a photo just as it is, without any manipulation, but exploring the options can lead to some intriguing results.) Here are some tips to consider when choosing a photo:

+ Look for a photo that has contrast in colors, shades of color (color values), or shapes. The photo Becka used (right) had a wide range of colors.

+ Look for a photo that shows texture. The texture of the yarn in Becka's photo adds depth to the image.

+ Don't be too literal. Look beyond the "what it is" of the image to see interesting shapes or areas of the image that might make a good design. Look at the image from a few feet away and see how it might look different than it does up close. Alternatively, zoom in so that you are just looking at a section of the image out of context.

+ Think about the end use. Is the placement of an element in the photo going to draw attention to something you would rather not emphasize? For instance, if you are making a skirt, you might not want lines pointing to your hips.

+ Check the file size. Ideally your photo will be somewhere around 25 to 30 inches (63.5 to 76.2 cm) at 150 ppi / 3750 to 4500 pixels square. Depending on how you manipulate the photo and the look you are trying to achieve, you might be happy with a file smaller than that, knowing that it may look more pixelated when it prints. Sometimes you can cheat a bit with resolution, depending on the result you are trying to achieve.

ABOVE Through the "magic" of filters, Becka transformed a simple photo of yarn on shelves into an exciting fabric.

designing the fabric

Note: It is helpful to decide which fabric you want to print your skirt on before you do the final design. Each fabric has a different width and that will determine whether you can fit both the front and back of the skirt on 1 yard (.9 m) of fabric or if you need to lay out and print on 2 separate yards (2 m) of fabric. For this example, Becka worked with a fabric that is 54 inches (137.2 cm) wide and both the front and back fit on 1 yard (.9 m) of fabric.

10 Set up the file and place image.
Becka made her skirt in linen-cotton canvas, so she created a new Photoshop file that was 54 x 36 inches (137.2 x 91 cm) / 8100 by 5400 pixels. Select and place the photo image that you have chosen to work with; put it anywhere on the canvas. The photo will be on its own layer in the Layers palette.

11 Manipulate the photo with filters.
Filters can soften sharp edges, add texture and interest, and generally transform a photo in many intriguing ways. You can layer filters on top of one another to create even more effects. Many photo programs include all kinds of filters.

Go to the "Filter" menu item and choose "Filter Gallery." Becka chose the "Cutout" filter and adjusted the settings in the panel that popped up until she had a result she liked. She also applied a Warp effect to the photo to bend the lines from the photo to match the curve of the skirt. Click OK to apply the filter (Figures 10 and 11).

12 Cut out your skirt shape.

Once you are finished manipulating the image, it is time to "cut out" the skirt shape from the photo. In Illustrator, open the skirt pattern document from earlier and select the skirt shape. Copy, switch to Photoshop, and paste this shape as a new layer in the Photoshop document. Choose "Pixels" from the dialog box that pops up (Figure 12).

Now look at your photo layer. The photo should cover the entire skirt shape layer that you just placed. Move the photo layer and skirt shape so that they appear right on top of each other and are aligned the way you like. You may need to adjust the size of your photo layer at this point so that it fits the skirt. Use the transform command to allow you to resize just that layer. Caution: Do *not* adjust the size of your skirt shape layer or the finished skirt will not fit you!

In the Layers palette (the panel for adjusting layers), drag the skirt shape layer so it appears *below* the photo layer (Figure 13).

FIGURE 10 Photoshop has many Filters and Effects that can change the look of your photo, such as add texture or make it more abstract.

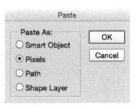

FIGURE 11 The Warp effect can be used to bend a horizontal line to match the curve of the skirt.

FIGURE 12 When you paste the skirt shape into a new layer, choose the Pixel option.

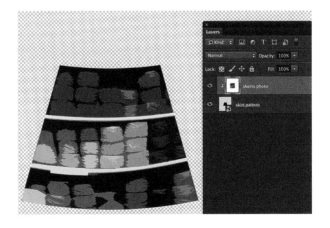

FIGURE 13 Arrange the layers in the Layers palette with the photo on top and the skirt shape layer on the bottom.

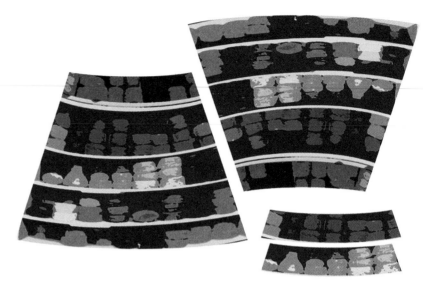

FIGURE 14 Right click the photo layer and choose "Create Clipping Mask" to cut away extra parts of photo and leave the skirt shape.

FIGURE 15 Duplicate your shapes to create two skirt panels and two facing pieces and place on your canvas.

Click the right side of the mouse (right-click or option-click) on the *photo layer* and choose "Create Clipping Mask" from the pop-up menu (Figure 14). This will cut away everything that you don't need and leave you with exactly the skirt shape cut out from your photo.)

13 Duplicate to make front and back.

Duplicate the shape you made in Step 12 to make the other half of the skirt. In the Layers palette, select both the photo layer and the skirt shape layer. Right-click (option-click) on one of the layers and choose "Merge Layers" from the menu that pops up. This will combine the two into one layer. Then right-click (option-click) again on the new merged layer and choose "Duplicate Layer." This will make a copy for the other half of the skirt.

Use the Move tool to move this new layer around to fit it on the canvas. You may need to rotate it so it will fit in the space. With the duplicate layer selected in the Layers Palette, go to the "Edit" menu, choose "Transform," and then choose "Rotate 180°."

14 Repeat to make the facing pieces.

Repeat Steps 12 and 13 to "cut out" and place your waistband facing pieces. Make two waistband facing pieces and place them on your canvas in the available space (Figure 15).

Note: If the two skirt pieces don't fit on the 1-yard (.9 m) Photoshop canvas, then lay out just one half of the skirt (one skirt, one waistband facing) and print 2 yards (2 m) of that design.

15 Save and upload.

We recommend that you first save this file as a .psd (Photoshop) format so that you can make revisions later to the layers if necessary. When you are ready to upload and print, save it as a .jpg. Choose your fabric and order 1 to 2 yards (.9 to 2 m) as determined in Step 14.

making the skirt

16 Prepare the fabric.

Wash and dry the fabric. Press it to remove any wrinkles. Cut out the skirt and facing pieces along the printed edges. Since Becka built a seam allowance into the design, you don't need to cut with extra space. The more accurately you cut, the easier your skirt will go together. Use a zigzag or overlock stitch, or a serger, to finish all of the raw edges of the skirt and facing pieces.

17 Stitch the side seams.

With right sides facing, match up the side seams on the right side of the skirt and pin. On the left side, match the top edge of the zipper tape to the waistband edge of the skirt. Mark with a pin at ¼ inch (6 mm) above the zipper stop at the bottom, then set aside the zipper. Match the remaining left side seams and pin.

Stitch each side seam using a ½-inch (1.2 cm) seam allowance. On the side with the zipper, stitch from the hem edge to the pin marking the end of the zipper. Backstitch to reinforce the stitching. Switch the stitch length on your machine to the longest length (a basting stitch). Do not backstitch but continue to stitch from the zipper stop mark to the waistband of the skirt. (Be sure to switch the stitch length back

to normal as soon as you are finished with this step.)

18 Insert the zipper.

Press the side seam allowances open. With the zipper closed, pin it face down onto the wrong side of the basted side seam, with the zipper teeth centered over the seam. Match the top edge of the zipper tape to the top edge of the waistband. Pin in place. Hand-baste the zipper in place and then remove the pins.

Switch to the zipper foot on your sewing machine. Stitch down the side of the zipper, across the bottom, and up the other side, keeping your stitches close to the zipper teeth. Use the seam ripper to pull out the basting stitches along the zipper portion of the side seam and remove any stray threads. Press.

19 Add the waistband facing.

Stitch the right side seam of the facing and press the seam allowances open. Matching the right side of the facing to the right side of the skirt, pin the facing to the waistband edge, matching the side seam.

Stitch the waistband edge with a ½-inch (1.2 cm) seam allowance, catching the top edges of the zipper tape in the stitching.

Press the waistband seam allowance toward the facing. Understitch the facing by stitching through the seam

allowance and the facing piece, ¼ inch (6 mm) from the waist seamline. Press the facing to the inside of the skirt.

Turn under ½ inch (1.2 cm) at the short ends of the facing and slipstitch them to the back of the zipper tape. Add a few stitches to secure the right side of the facing to the right side seam of the skirt to keep it in place. Handstitch a hook-and-eye closure to the very top edge of the zipper.

20 Hem the skirt with bias tape.

Becka hemmed her skirt with bias tape because she likes how it adds an extra pop of color. (If you prefer not to use bias tape, simply make a narrow hem by machine.) To hem with bias tape, unfold one long edge of the bias tape. Match this unfolded raw edge of the bias tape to the bottom edge of the skirt, right sides together. Pin in place, overlapping the bias tape slightly at the ends. Trim the extra bias tape.

Stitch all the way around the hem, following the original foldline of the bias tape. Press the bias tape away from the skirt and then fold it to the inside of the skirt along the stitching line. Pin in place.

Stitch once more very close to the upper folded edge of the bias tape. Press to set the curve.

TEST YOUR EYE!

It's time for your Repeat Quiz! Put all the things you've learned to the test by trying to identify each of the repeat layouts used at right. Look at each of the images and decide if the repeat is basic, half-drop, half-brick, or mirror. To refresh your memory, go to page 60. Then, decide if it is simple (you can see the grid) or seamless. You may want to revisit the little trick we taught on page 62 about identifying seamless repeats. (Turn to page 204 for the answers.)

Why do you do this? Because looking at other designs can help you be a better designer. Looking at the repeat for a design you like might give you an idea about how to create that feeling in your own design.

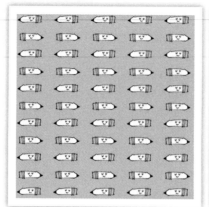

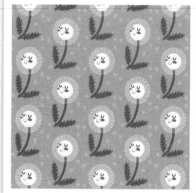

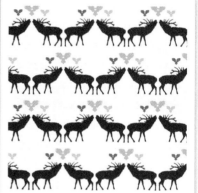

PRACTICE: WE HEART VECTORS!

In Chapter 10 (page 160) we introduced vectors. To practice making a vector, try drawing a simple heart.

1 Open a new canvas.

2 Click with the Pen tool to make the point at the bottom of the heart.

3 Place the next pin to change the line direction at the side where a heart needs to curve. Click at the left side to place the pin, holding down the mouse and dragging the cursor. You will see the line start to curve and two little handles will appear attached to your pin. Don't worry about what the curve looks like or where the handles are right now—you'll adjust later (Figure 1).

4 Continue around the heart shape, clicking and dragging to place a pin at the top left of the heart, at the dimple, the top right, the right side, and finally clicking to connect with the very first pin you placed to close the shape (6 pins total; Figure 2).

5 Once you have the shape roughed out, use the handles on each pin to adjust the curves. Click each pin with the Direct Select tool to make the handles appear. Click one of the round knobs on the ends of the handle and drag it to adjust the curve; try using each handle to see how the changes affect your drawing. Work your way around the heart to adjust the shape as you like it (Figure 3).

You can change the curve in many ways:

+ Push the knob closer to the pin to shrink the curve or pull it farther away to make it bulge out.

+ Push the handles all the way in toward the pin to make a sharp point.

+ Click the pins themselves to move them around and the lines will stretch to fit.

6 When you are finished adjusting the shape, fill it with color by clicking the shape with the Select tool. You can choose both the fill color and the outline color in the color palette (Figure 4).

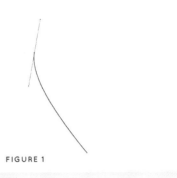

FIGURE 1

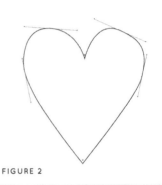

FIGURE 2

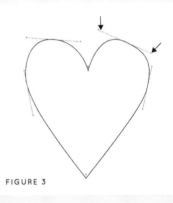

FIGURE 3

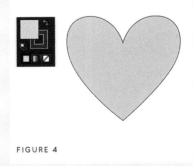

FIGURE 4

TEST YOUR EYE! (ANSWERS)

For each design, one possible repeat tile is outlined. For many designs, there is more than one way to create a repeat tile.

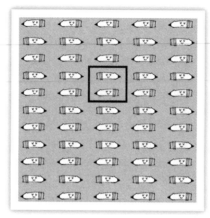

basic, simple
Smile Pencils, Anda Corrie (anda)

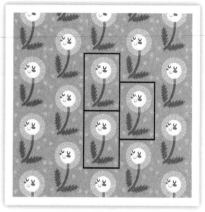

half-drop, seamless
Dandelions, Heidi Kenney (heidikenney)

basic, seamless
Geometry Gold, Alicia Vance (alicia_vance)

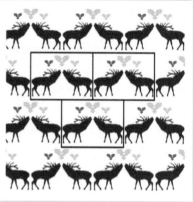

half-brick, simple
Forest, Isabelle Kunz (troismiettes)

basic, seamless
Citrus Abundance 3 Pink Fruit, Vincent Desjardins (vinpauld)

basic, seamless
Snaking This Way and That, Samarra Khaja (sammyk)

PATTERN PIECES FOR FAMILY PORTRAITS NECKTIE (PAGE 132)

To use these pattern pieces, first photocopy this page at 100% and cut out each rectangular area (as shown by the white background). Then, photocopy each rectangular piece at 400%. Each rectangular area should fit on an 8½ x 11-inch piece of paper. All of these pieces are cut from the tie fabric. To make the front tie pattern piece, tape together A, B, and C in that order, matching the diamonds on each piece. To make the tie back pattern piece, tape together D, E, and F in that order. The dotted line on each piece indicates the fold line and also the cutting line for the tie interlining (cut from wool flannel). The arrows on each piece indicate the grain line. The seam allowances are included in the pieces.

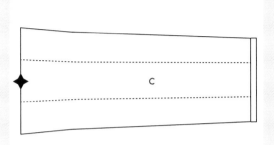

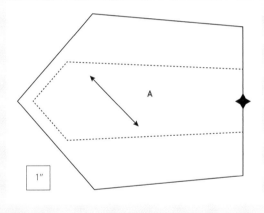

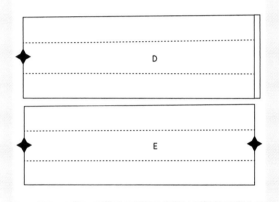

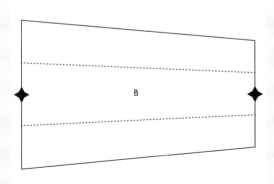

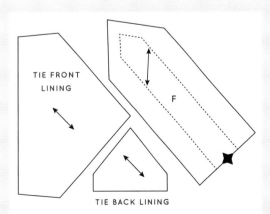

CHOOSING SOFTWARE PROGRAMS

There are a number of software programs for designing textiles and papers, and choosing the ones that suit your needs best, especially when you are just starting out, can be challenging. We've explored numerous programs and rounded up our favorites here, from Adobe products to free programs.

When looking for software, the first decision to make is whether you want to work with raster or vector images. Raster images are made up of a set grid of dots called pixels, while vector images are based off simple geometric shapes such as lines, curves, and points. Adobe Photoshop is an example of a raster-based program, while Adobe Illustrator works with vector images.

You also have the option to purchase design software or use an open-source option. Open-source design programs are free to use and are either downloadable or accessible through the program's website.

The programs listed here offer a range of capabilities, from novice to expert.

ADOBE PHOTOSHOP is a robust graphics editor that works primarily with raster images (pixels), allowing users to create their own images or easily edit photographs. Photoshop contains a ton of tools with a range of functions, offering new users the ability to really grow their skills to the level of professionals. With Photoshop, designers can easily select colors or groups of pixels to manipulate very fine details of any image in a myriad of different ways. Many industry designers work in Photoshop, giving them the opportunity to learn and grow. Adobe now gives designers the option to purchase a monthly subscription rather than buying the program outright.

PICMONKEY is an open-source web-based editing tool that gives users the ability to create images from scratch or edit photographs. While this is a relatively powerful tool, it doesn't allow users the ability to do quite as much as other tools, like Photoshop. For example, you won't be able to go back in and edit font size/color once you've saved your finished PicMonkey file—your changes will be final. This is a great resource if you're looking to add basic text, colorful, cute stamps, or graphic icons to your image. We recommend this program for beginners creating simple designs with geometric shapes, text-based designs, adding text to existing designs, or creating a master file with multiple images.

GIMP, OR GNU IMAGE MANIPULATION PROGRAM, is

a free program that's great for editing and resizing photos, combining multiple images into one file, adding text to images, and adjusting colors. For a free program, it packs a punch and can do many of the things Photoshop can, but because it's an open-source program, it has a slightly steeper learning curve and less professional interface than Photoshop. We recommend this program for intermediate designers interested in editing existing images on a budget.

PIXLR is another image editing software program that's great for photos and existing images, rather than for creating new ones from scratch. With filters, frames, text, and even the ability to overlay and combine two different photos into one image, it's similar to PicMonkey with a focus on editing existing photographs, not resizing them or creating a seamless repeat. There are several different versions you can choose from based on your needs.

ADOBE ILLUSTRATOR is a vector-based design program (as opposed to raster-based) that allows users to create original artwork that can be resized and easily manipulated. The latest version of this software also has the tools necessary for creating unique repeat textile patterns. Start with a blank canvas or use a scan of hand-drawn art to get started. Using the Pen tool, it's easy to "trace" over scanned artwork, bringing to life a sketch that may have started out with just pencil and paper. Illustrator is a powerful tool that many professional designers choose for fabric design.

INKSCAPE is a free alternative to Adobe Illustrator. Like other open-source programs, Inkscape isn't quite as user-friendly as its more expensive competitors, but has a plethora of powerful drawing and designing tools. If you don't have an image already and are starting with a blank canvas, Inkscape can help you create editable shapes and freehand lines to draw your image. If you're trying to make a simple design or trace a hand-drawn design with digital lines and don't want to pay for Adobe Illustrator, Inkscape is a great option. If you're hoping to create simple designs that are digitized from the get-go, or images that will fill a yard or more, this tool is for you.

REPPER is an online program from the Netherlands that gives users simple digital tools to make repeat patterns for use on fabrics, stationery, and more. They offer a free demo to play around with, or you can purchase the full program, which allows you to export higher-quality files. You start out by uploading any digital file from your computer, selecting a portion of it, then use a selection tool to create super fun Kaleidoscope-esque repeating patterns.

Repper then allows you to export a repeating tile, or the entire surface selection. A ton of fun for beginning surface-design artists wanting to create something truly original.

SEAMLESS LITE is an online open-source tool created by the popular color palette website ColourLovers. This tool makes it super easy to design great-looking vector patterns for textile design projects. With simple editing tools you can resize, rotate, and add shapes, lines, and text to the canvas and it tiles automatically. Once you're ready to select a color palette for your creation, Seamless integrates smoothly with the ColourLovers interface so you can create a unique color palette for your repeating design and name it. Save your pattern template and share it with the world, or send it directly to your Spoonflower library.

ADOBE COLOR is a web-based tool where users can create and save color palettes that can be easily translated to patterns created in other design programs. This is particularly useful when creating a range of designs to ensure the same colors are used throughout the collection.

The best and most obvious ways to source images to print on Spoonflower—which are well covered in this book—are these:

+ Create your own designs, either digitally or on paper, the old-fashioned way. Images on paper can be scanned and, if you're not an artist, there is still a lot you can do using digital photos from your camera or phone.

+ Find designs by artists who have made their work available to purchase in the Spoonflower marketplace. The next best thing to being an artist is supporting indie artists!

Having covered the obvious, the Internet does offer many amazing resources for downloading images that can be used as the basis for projects, including some of the projects in this book. There are, however, a few very important caveats to understand before you think about using images from the Internet:

+ The vast majority of images on the Internet CANNOT be used, despite the fact that you may be able to download them to your computer. Printing an image that is not your own, even if it's something common like the Mona Lisa, is not okay without some kind of explicit permission or license granting you the right to reproduce the image for your own purposes.

+ When you do have some indication that an image is okay for use by virtue of its license, or because it is in the public domain, it is still not okay to represent that image as your own work. To the degree that it is possible, you should credit the original artist and source if you are displaying the work in any public form or on your own website.

+ The right to use an image that is not your own is not the same as the right to sell that image or products bearing that image. Many images are made available for sharing and use in personal projects, but not commercial ones. The default assumption should be that a public domain image can be used for a personal project but not for a commercial one.

Here are some good places to start if you are looking for images to use:

DOVER (www.doverpublications.com) publishes a series of books on pattern, including historic textile designs, that come with CDs full of artwork. Be aware that the images on the CDs are probably not set up to repeat neatly in tiles, so even if you upload a design from a Dover CD to Spoonflower, it may not work well in a quantity larger than a swatch. The Dover license is also restricted to personal use.

CREATIVE COMMONS (www.creativecommons.org) is an organization devoted to promoting the sharing and use of creative materials legally. It offers a search tool (http://search.creativecommons.org/) that allows people to find images with licenses that specially allow the re-use of images for personal use and, in some cases, commercial use. In all cases, however, be sure to credit your source and artist.

GETTY ART COLLECTION (www.getty.edu/art/collection/) offers thousands of images available for personal use from the J. Paul Getty Museum.

The Libraries and Information Services at Columbia University offer a web page with very good, basic overview of copyright as it relates to art and design: http://copyright.columbia.edu/copyright/special-topics/art-and-other-images/

Published in 2015 by
Stewart, Tabori & Chang

An imprint of ABRAMS

Text and illustrations
copyright © 2015 Spoonflower

Photographs copyright © 2015 Jenny
Hallengren (unless otherwise noted)

Photographs on pages 7, 8, 9, 84, 87,
107, and 160 by Joel and Ashley Selby/
This Paper Ship © 2015 Spoonflower

Page 76: Poster designed by
Tracy Jenkins, Village

Library of Congress Control Number:
978-1-61769-078-5
ISBN: 978-1-61769-078-5

Editor: Melanie Falick with Valerie Shrader
Designer: Sarah Gifford
Illustrator: Anda Corrie
Production Manager: Denise LaCongo

The text of this book was composed in
Proxima Nova, Eames Century Modern,
and Quicksand.

Printed and bound in the United States
10 9 8 7 6 5 4 3 2 1

Stewart, Tabori & Chang books are
available at special discounts when
purchased in quantity for premiums and
promotions as well as fundraising or
educational use. Special editions can also
be created to specification. For details,
contact specialsales@abramsbooks.com
or the address below.

ABRAMS
THE ART OF BOOKS SINCE 1949

115 West 18th Street
New York, NY 10011
www.abramsbooks.com

ACKNOWLEDGMENTS

This book would not be possible without the Spoonflower community. Thank you to all the community members who responded to our queries, contributed projects and ideas, and who continue to inspire so much creativity and fantastic design.

A big thanks to one of Spoonflower's first team members, Darci Moyers, for her enthusiasm in getting this project off the ground, and to Allie Tate for picking up the thread after Darci moved on. Many people were instrumental early on in the process, especially Joel and Ashley Selby of This Paper Ship—and, of course, Joy Tutela, who so wonderfully represented the book. Thanks to Melanie Falick for taking on this project and working hard to get it finished, to Valerie Shrader for editing the manuscript with a keen eye, and to Sarah Gifford, the designer. Thanks, too, to Dervla Kelly, who brought the original project to STC Craft.

As the book went through the editing process, some terrific projects, concepts, and instructions did not make it into the final draft, and we would like to acknowledge a few specific designers whose work was omitted for their help in developing the material that became *The Spoonflower Handbook*: Mathew & Matthea den Boer, Sharon Turner, Kelly Harmon, Jennifer Wambach, Samarra Khaja, Gina Sekelsky, Nancy Kers, Candy Joyce, Allison Kreft, Elizabeth Harrington, Donna Kallner, Cean Irminger, Jennifer Finan, and Linda Robertus.

Becka would like to personally thank Andy Rahn for love, wine, and technical support; Melisa Wahlstrom for making sure she could always be where she needed to be; and to her parents, who are both artists and educators, for showing her the footsteps to follow. She would also like to give a special thanks to all of the students from her "Spoonflower classes" at Textile Center in Minneapolis for their questions, ideas, and enthusiasm. And, finally, thanks to Judi Ketteler, who makes her sound smarter, funnier, and more articulate and has been a partner and friend throughout.

Judi would like to personally thank her mom, Mary Ketteler, for being the original sewer in her life, and her dad, Bert Ketteler, who passed away during the writing of this book, but who leaves an enormous creative legacy in her heart. Thanks to her husband, Allen Raines, for making ample amounts of coffee daily and chicken *tikka masala* when it was most needed. Finally, she would like to thank Becka Rahn, who is undoubtedly the best book co-author in the history of book co-authors and saved her bacon more than one time.

In addition to thanking Becka and Judi and all of the folks listed in the earlier acknowledgments, Stephen is indebted to the Spoonflower team, which consists of many dedicated, creative, and hardworking individuals who work like maniacs to get through the mountains of fabric, wallpaper, and gift wrap they print and ship every day, and who care deeply about the people to whom all those beautiful designs are being sent. He is also grateful to have two business partners, Gart Davis and Allison Polish, who supported this book project from start to finish.